The Way Home

The Way Home

Poems by

Michael Morical

Kelsay Books

Cover art: James McGarrell

ISBN 13: 978-0692565483

Kelsay Books
Aldrich Press
www.kelsaybooks.com

In Memoriam:

Ann McGarrell
(September 18, 1933–January 10, 2016)

The threads of autumn yield
jitter and scroop of silk.
Never too busy for love.

—from "Gwen & Other Poems"
By Ann McGarrell

Acknowledgments

Thank you to the journals below for publishing these poems, some of which have been revised:

The Antigonish Review: "Subway News," "*Crepúsculo*"
Barrow Street: "A Shrink in Therapy"
Burning Word: "Landscape"
California Quarterly: "Hoosier at a Taiwan Night Market"
Carolina Quarterly: "The Cure"
Chan Magazine: "Calcutta Offering"
Common Ground Review: "Pickled in Plum Fumes"
Glass: A Journal of Poetry: "Vermont"
The Hardy Review: "Viewing"
Language and Literature: "Salesman"
The Literary Bohemian: "The Belle of Osaka"
The New York Quarterly: "Torpedo Juice"
NYC Big City Lit: "Tributaries," "Our Mutual Friend,""MRI,"
    "Returning," "Waiting Room," "A Box of Fresh"
The Pedestal Magazine: "The Traveling Temple"
Rattapallax: "Fall"
Rogue Scholars: "Tofu Turkey Day"
The Same: "Taipei Moving Day," "Another Last Ride," "Dessert,"
    "Sharing a Mirror," "Botanical Gardens"

Thanks to the friends who helped edit the manuscript: Steve Ayer, Patricia Brody, Paola Corso, Scott Ezell, Cori Gabbard, Sybil Kollar, Ann McGarrell, Philip Miller, Allan Stevenson and Karen Swenson.

Contents

Landscape

Between waterfalls
a poem written in moss
grows on stone.
Ferns sprout
from words intertwined,
twisted shaggy,
hard to define
in the mist sustaining them.

A Shrink in Therapy

My dusty reflection,
why do you stare
at your shadow?
Has a coin dropped?
Do you hear the ineffable?
Does this view
complete an illusion
that completes your self?
Or are you hungry?
The fricassee would stew
in its own juices
if only you lit the stove,
raised your head,
turned your eyes
from the mirror.

The Cure

As the priest prescribed,
I write *endure*
on a strip of paper
and burn it in a glass.
When the flame expires,
I drown the ash
and drink through
the unburned scrap
catching in my throat.
Water, water, more water.
Nothing should have
missed the fire.
I gasp and cough,
fighting to expel
the obstruction
or swallow it.

Trilogy 1

face down in mud
the road turned
and I didn't

snow
filling footprints
I forget your name

tongue to tongue
a mutt drinks the pond
he's standing in

Dessert

After all-you-can-eat
mom and I stop
by the statue of Burger
Chief in the parking lot—
his headdress sanded down
to the brown
of his never-painted skin.
In the shadow at his feet
we watch the after-
glow across the street:
the evanescence
of a rusty strip mall,
the amber shade
of a green elm.
We stand still
together, elapsing
with the sun.
Street lights flicker on.

Tributaries

Shopping list in mind:
mushrooms, Drano, mousetrap and thyme.
A cart rams my heel.
I page the circular
left in my basket.
The breeze of a butcher
rushing by touches my bare legs
as something clicks
and the produce is misted
and music rolls down the aisle
with the shopping carts
and everything missing fits
and the song passes through my hands
until I name it.

In the Recession

When Dad's teeth were falling out and his business stank,
he vowed to privatize our backyard over the septic tank.
He would build a fence like the Millers across the ditch
and buy a set of iron lawn chairs on layaway. We three
would lounge outdoors as a family. No one would
see us. Neither the trees in Dad's path nor the wagging
of Mom's index finger stopped him. He dug holes,
filled them with cement and planted his pickets.
But there were gaps where any motorist could see Mom
clipping coupons in her secondhand bikini. Dad said
trees filled the spaces in his fence. Before I could
challenge him, Mom shushed me with a glance.
That summer she sunbathed in her blue lawn chair
with broken straps. The recession had nothing
to do with us.

Downsizing

We postdate checks,
forgive debts,
splash the dust
so it stays
on the floor.
Don't be bashful.
Throw your cigarette
butts in the corner.
Never mind
the mattress
leaning on the wall.
It may look as if
we never unpacked,
as if we have nothing
worth packing, as
if you should demand
cash up front.
But we're incorporated.
See the inscription
on our brass plaque?
We paid good money
for that.

Aunt Betty

She deconstructs our house
whenever whimsy dictates;
bookcases crammed with super
hero comics were torn apart today.

Whichever whimsy takes her
hides Mother's scissors again.
Hulk and Spiderman are ripped apart,
recycled or stashed in the closet.

I find Mother's scissors deep
in a kitchen drawer left ajar
as Betty shuffles bundles
of *Time, Life and Vogue*.

In the kitchen drawer
I find some screws I lost.
The stacks of *Vogue, Time* and *Life*
are asymmetric in Betty's eye.

As I gather more screws,
she stands on a TV box,
seeking symmetry in her eye,
one vision that might stay put.

She wobbles on the box
and reaches deep for a design,
a vision that might stay put.
All plans sift through her hands.

Betty reaches deep for stuff
to stuff the bookcases she spared.
So many plans sifting through
her hands reconstruct our home.

Waiting Room

I have a rash.
What are you in for?
I wish you'd find
whatever's at the bottom
of your bag, whatever
makes you dig through
things you don't take out.
Are you afraid I'll see?
My whole apartment's like that,
all I've been and didn't trash.
I may be contagious so I keep
my hands off the magazines.
Can you tell?
Either you've found the shape
you seek or given up looking.
Now you're pretending to sleep?
Why don't we talk?
Words could air us out.
I search my mind
for something I knew,
something that fits you.
And the nurse
calls my name.

Maiden Voyage

Looking for my keys, I find Grandma's
honeymoon pictures. She climbs rocks
bleached by sun and time, her parasol
aimed at the groom or a Sacred Fig rooted
in stone. Her way forward floods the photos.
Grandpa broods in the opposite corner,
clearly out of focus. But a steely bearing
makes his monkey suit even spiffier
as he waits for the bride to finish.
Is his honeymoon on the rocks? The tale ends
as if it ran out of film: bride on a cliff,
groom's eyes keen on his pocket watch.
My husband yells to hurry, or the freshest
day-old donut holes will be gone.

The Traveling Temple

Altar in a suitcase:
creased photos
of Osho, Sai Baba and Che,
a disassembled platform,
candles, incense, lace;
Krishna, Kali, Christ
and other cartooned gods
whose picture frames
klankety-klank as Kevin
walks the plank from boat
to dock, stopping
where the board sags,
teetering over the bay—
the weight of God
in one sweaty hand,
the other empty.
He squeezes his slippery
handle and prays for balance
prophet by prophet,
deity by deity,
with extra entreaties
to Our Lady of Guadalupe.
The pantheon is heavy.
There's no one left to beg
so he begs them all
in one heavy breath
and a guy loading durians
onto another boat smirks
out loud: *You, you go.*
Kevin walks the line,
thanking the angel
who hurls spiked fruit
one at a time.

Hoosier at a Taiwan Night Market

I stroll down the lane
of tapioca tea, used power tools,
grilled giblets, Confucian classics
and plastic ducks.
Vendors line both sides,
each stand with a generator
humming juice through a clear
glass bulb. Grateful for sundown,
yet still wavy from the heat,
I chew my squid,
walking scattered thoughts.

Then something flashes out
from the guava guy's shadow
and gassy breath embraces me.
It's the town drunk
and his grip is tight. Wriggling
to break it, I dance him around
to a jingle guaranteeing
the sweetest, freshest guavas in town.

People watch between spoonfuls
of catfish soup. A guy
auctioning seafood by the frisbee-full
huffs into his microphone:
Big nose and stinky ghost
do the tango!

When I hug my partner,
he lets me go.

Trilogy 2

a busker makes
me play his violin
scratching the ice

free jazz
I'm paid
to move my drums

chainsaws harmonize
a pack of dogs
eyes the sun

Meditation on the Ground Floor

A radio down the hall blares
Michael Jackson's *Human
Nature* as, step by step,
I try to focus on all I hear,
not just the Basie Band
blasting a blues in my head.
Several blocks away,
sirens fade and crescendo.
Miss Chi downstairs dates
disaster in a checkered suit.
The old folks outside
my window get her knocked
up by sheer imagination.
Then my fridge clicks off.

As the dumpling vendor
pedals his bicycle closer,
the tape loop of his forlorn
call to eat gets louder,
harder to resist.
Closer to home, old grouch Chang
drops his marbles one by one
and they roll to a standstill
on the floor above my ceiling.
A guy whose voice cuts
through soundproofing
joins the busybodies outside.
He witnessed Miss Chi's
beau, a militant vegan,
buying chitlins at market.
*Pregnant women love
chitlins*, he announces.
The sirens scream along

with Chinese musettes
in a funeral procession.
Miss Chi herself hums
along with the radio
as she leaves the building
solo: *We are the World.*

Calcutta Offering

Naked in solid rain,
she washes a taxi
with her tattered dress,
rubbing hard,
tensing noodle arms.

At the end,
when the sun
is drying her
and the taxi driver
has pitched her a coin,
this trembling child
climbs into
her ashen washcloth
and buys a cup of tea.

She spills some
in the gutter
and offers the rest to me.

Taipei Moving Day

After your Dad shook
the toilet brush in your face,
you left home for a room
above the Stewed Goose
Roost on Movie Street.
Neon signs flashed
through frosted windows,
strobing the emptiness.
The old tenant left no
bulbs in the sockets.

Our voices echoed
off the total lack of furniture.
The only decoration was
a bust of Augustus
we called handsome boy.
You wore a homemade night-
gown cut like a flour sack.
We locked the door,
ate mooncakes and lay
on the floor. Tiles cooled
our skin. We rolled
in the soup of the heat,
laughing, grinding our knees—
one shadow in a flash,
one flash of the strobe.

Pickled in Plum Fumes

Jilted at harvest, Ueki took a room
in the matchmaker's house by the plum trees.
He carried his father's suitcase through the perfume
of that autumn's last fruit fermenting on the ground.
He would not offer to pick the sweet, dark orbs
the next year or any year. Every fall he squatted
just out the cherry-wood door, breathing fumes
of fruit-come-wine until they went to his head.
Then he watched the moon through clouds and night.
A smell of straw from old *tatamis* tinged
the closet-sized room where Ueki kept himself,
emerging only to eat at his Mom's until the plums
ripened, fell and turned to wine each autumn.
His drunkenness was orderly. When the matchmaker
was carted off to a booby hatch, Ueki snored under
the plum tree with the thickest perfume. It was that
time of year. He didn't hear the matchmaker's pickle
jars break as the medics restrained her. He didn't
smell the black and sour juice that spilled. And he never
gave up his room.

The Belle of Osaka

On leave from the sanatorium,
I wander my dead mother's house, nibble
plums and radishes she pickled herself,
unpack kimonos saved for my nuptials—
the only match she couldn't make.
Mother emerges from my wedding garb,
chiding the daughter no one would marry.
If only I hadn't stuttered, slouched
or blotched my makeup, if only I'd waltzed
like Princess Grace, spoken French and played Chopin;
I'd have matched the whims of any man.
But my quaking hands suggest another fate.
Soon this house will be emptied and wrecked.
What could have been survives my mother's death.

Returning

A bus drops
me at my doorstep
where the evening paper
is ready to unfold.
Sitting on the stoop,
I hesitate
while there's still light,
while echoes of echoes
throb behind my eyes.
It's TV time.
What must be news
flickers out
a neighbor's window
onto the sidewalk.
Where are my glasses?
I squint at
violets in the grass,
cracks in my driveway,
a trike parked
just where fancy
left it—
no keys in my pocket,
the windows barred.

By a Bistro Window

As she waits for
the early-bird special
to begin, her brother
passes in traffic,
steering with his knees,
grinning into
a greasy hero
that fills both hands
and leaks.

He sways to music
she can't hear.
His Thunderbird roars
when he touches
the gas, penetrating
the bistro window.
Who needs a muffler?

By the time she waves,
he's turned a corner.

Botanical Gardens

The cherry blossoms online,
updated in real time,
are missing from the groves.
I get my first mosquito bite
of spring as I compose
in sagging clouds
a scalding email
to whom it didn't concern.
My fingers itch for a keyboard.
But it's misting,
the damn squirrels are squawking
and my Mac is tucked
in its waterproof pouch.

As the drizzle thickens,
the frogs come out,
each leaping
through the glint of its skin,
and it's hard to walk
without squashing one
so I stop on the squishy,
manicured lawn.
Who cares why I came?
It's pouring.

Vermont

Two boys
walk the railroad,
picking a bucket
of raspberries one by one—
violets between the tracks.

A Box of Fresh

In the last pitch black
before dawn
the baker would leave
a box of donuts
on the grocery's back stoop.
You could bite
into that smell, especially
if you'd missed dinner.
We'd snatch the glazed
and quarts of milk
from neighbors' boxes,
switching victims daily.
Cops turned a blind eye.

As the sun came up,
we'd wash down our donuts
with milk and hop a freight train,
riding just to go.
We lied
about ladies in the bordello
when we didn't know
the basics of plumbing.
Our guts full,
we'd ride
as far as Delphi, Indiana
and hitchhike home.

Relocating (Meet me at the Airport)

I wore a suit,
a sweater
and a parka.
You pushed the cart
of all I owned
to a blue bus stop.
We had the whole
double-decker
to ourselves.
Twilight dimmed
through tinted windows
and lace curtains
as the white-gloved
driver announced
the stops he skipped.
We looked at each other
in the darkening glow:
the place to be,
the place to go.

Trilogy 3

sharing a love seat
the newlyweds
text each other

bare trees
in April drizzle
the hush you left

family photo
your face cut out
and taped back in

Fall

When these leaves were buds, we argued commas.
Insisting on semicolons or full stops
between ideas, I whined and nothing calmed me.
For micro-points of ink my nerves would pop.
One night I caught a ride on Mingus music.
I grabbed the swinging pendulum and swayed,
losing grammar, stealing bliss from movement.
Propulsion made pedantic static fade.
Then you led me tingling through a barbed-wire fence
to Kinsey's backyard. By a dildo fountain
we cut our minds and let our bodies dance.
Dipped and done, we parsed a moonlit mountain.
Now our brittle colors fall with towers.
The rocking change was never really ours.

Note on the Fridge

Happy crescent moon!
I'm sorry I picked
all your kumquats.
They taste like perfume.
I didn't know you'd trim
your Christmas tree
exclusively
with these unchewables.
So please forgive me;
I've eaten every one.

Tofu Turkey Day

The oven is broken so I freeze the Tofurkey
with the gluten-jerky wishbone that pulls like taffy.
But the kids need to sink their teeth into
something besides themselves. At freezer's bottom
I find the mini-flank of soy beef I didn't broil
last Christmas. It looks nothing like beans.
The blood is bloodless. I carve it with a hacksaw,
punch holes in the strips and fill them
with sesame oil, burgundy and pine nuts.
Through two football games, the toaster
oven melts this disguise into a viscous pool
of beef—medium-well when cooled.
The children chew themselves to sleep.

How I Lost Your Poems

Your book arrived in extra padding
the morning I went to Jones Beach.
I stuffed it in my daypack
to read your sonnets by the sea,
to ride the meter riding me.

But first I swam, having stashed your work
in my waterproof pack where a box of blueberries
spilled a summer or two ago,
blotching my *New Yorker* cover, torn
from the rest, of course, by rummaging.

And while I breast-stroked back to shore,
a seagull pecked your poems, tearing
lines, ripping images, swallowing words.
What can I tell you?
How had a birdbrain unzipped the zipper?

When the thief sensed my urgency,
it grabbed a wad of verse
in its beak and flew out with the undertow.
Who knows where it landed, or if?
Can you send another copy?

Our Mutual Friend

Jangle-jangle, the anklets he gave you
rang my bell each step. Why did you shake them
like a metronome ticking me to death?
Why did you read me your lover's letters?
He sent me his Dickens soaked and dried,
a warped reminder of things as they stood,
or didn't. You jingled my nightmares.
I wouldn't leave until you bought your ticket.
That time grows louder in echoes, jingle-jingle.
Every chime makes me spin and ring
until I ask why. Why am I holding on?
I wish the racket would put me to sleep,
seeking distraction in Trojans and Greeks:
Those wounds heal ill that men do give themselves.

—Last line from William Shakespeare's *Troilus and Cressida*

Fatima's Gift

After my wife left,
I ate a cold salad on a cold night.
The greens were yellow,
the tomato white.
My homemade dressing
had congealed.
Then the doorbell
punctured the silence.
Outside bars and glass,
my neighbor stood in a maroon sari.
I opened the door and she handed me
a bowl of *keer*, sweet porridge
with coconut, peanuts and raisins.
It warmed my numb fingers.
You eat, she said, smiling
above her scarf.

Into the Looking Glass

After she moved her garden,
the violets returned.
Waves of April mornings
flooded the cobwebs,
laying the wind thick.
Whatever it planted thrived
in the topsoil she left him.

He sat in the colors
and turned a lighter shade
of the night she emptied all day.
Moonset took him in.
He asked the sky
where darkness lies
when buds have gone away,
how the sun shattered the horizon
he'd made of her missing fingerprints.

The architecture crept up on him like old age,
like the gilding of mirrors in gilded frames.
Dandelions brought out the weed in him,
turning his head to fuzz
that blew through her jasmine
without sticking.

Torpedo Juice

No booze on board, sailors tap a torpedo,
draining enough fuel for cocktail hour.
One expert claims the navy overloads
its missiles to sweeten seamen going sour.
Otherwise, who would man this floating brig
a captain parks on the buffered side of war?
Those who doubt their mission take to the gig
with a drink or two. Survivors don't need lore.
To change the pace, they taste some shaving lotion
poured through sliced bread to filter poison.
It bites like Wild Turkey. The boys imagine
ground to dance on, babes and happy noise.
Someday they'll follow a destroyer home.
A seaman hoots and watches twilight moan.

Crepúsculo

Half past crystal,
the sailor's eyes
inhabit the seagull,
wishing for no land
in sight, settling for
a river he won't cross.

MRI

In a slide show of my brain
the mind loses mystery fast.
What processes the world
processes itself:
a network of hardware
wrapped in insulation
with gaps where it's supposed
to fit snug against my skull—
no eternity,
no palm tree,
no copies of the love
I've made.

I was expecting 3-D
or at least one cavern
that spirals somewhere
I can't fathom,
no matter how dinky,
obstructed by its own turns,
memories
spilling through each other,
poised for dreams
to bring them out.

Instead, Dr. Chow clicks
her mouse on a sequence
of flat views
as she sips coffee, assuring me
the gaps in my gray matter
don't indicate atrophy.

Reservation

The hemlock lady mails
me a final exit kit:
enough helium
to make this scrap
heap float.
I store her gift.
Tomorrow tingles
like twilight
in a heat wave.
I am *not* dying.

Sharing a Mirror

Get me some coffee—black! I think
I've changed my mind about living another day.
Thank you, son, for spending the gaping night.
I heard you snore when the whirlpool
of fire sucked and burned, spinning me upside down.
My lifetime of sense was breaking apart.
But in your breath I found my own.
The ending stopped and left me a mirror.
It holds my ashen face and yours—two loners.
Son, you've sat here till your butt's gone numb,
ridden herd on my doctors, fed me avocado.
God knows you'll have a chance to take me home.
But who will prop you up when your body breaks
down? Whose breath will you share?

Another Last Ride

The day after Christmas, when our plastic spruce is flattened, packed and returned to the attic, Dad feels a hundred percent better, he says, clinking the ice in his gimlet. *It's all over but the shoutin'*, he yawns, *and that ain't too damn loud.* We sigh together breath to breath, happy we don't have to be happy, happy the dancing Santa's stored.

Neighbors burn their trees the night I leave, the glow lighting Dad's couch. He sings of Minnie the Mermaid's deep-sea bungalow, recites the lines I love from his college days: *My favorite pastime after dark/ is goosing statues in the park.* His spirit sprawls around me: the once-mighty handshake, the car trunk full of gin, the coffee cans brimming with cigarette butts, the X-rays always clear. Can I leave again?

I scrub the toilet, dust the chandelier and watch him doze. Dad's more tired more often than last trip. On the way to the airport, steering with an index finger, he remembers yet again that Mom bathed me in the kitchen sink, that I peed on a pot roast. *Damn kid*, he chuckles. And the Dodge just glides.

Subway News

A woman in satin yells
Oh Shit at her tabloid.
Her seat won't hold
this wrath. She rises,
waving the *Post*,
swatting the outrage.
She spins and crescendos:
Oh shit no!
In sync with a battery man,
I roll my eyes, keeping a hand
on the tape-covered
box between my legs.
She stomps once, finds
another seat and grimaces
back at the paper:
Oh honey no!
Her voice fades
as pages turn.

Salesman

After death his secrets came out.
The man in the blanks grew a body
of smoke and secondhand accounts.
Details clashed. Portraits were spotty.
The florist he punched hit him back.
Mornings he sold patented selves
then golfed with his friend, the twelve-pack.
Rinsing with coffee cut the smell,
but only alerted his wife.
He knew she knew. She played along.
She never guessed he kept a knife
or wore a blue batik sarong.
Not afraid to hear the worst,
the widow of rumors kissed his corpse.

Parting Words

You look better dead than you did alive:
no hundred-proof breath, no smirk, no red eye.
You never shut up, never blushed this pink.
Maybe booze preserves. What's pickled doesn't stink.
Here's a little flask for your pocket.
In cold storage you'll need some tonic
to take the edge off, to keep the shakes at bay,
to laugh at the worms that eat your decay.
I've wished you dead, tried to lose what you lacked.
You snorted all our coke behind my back.
The "Ecstasy" you stole and sold the cops
was caffeine. You couldn't ever stop
devouring prospects and hatching scams.
I could have better spared a better man.

  —Last line from William Shakespeare's Henry IV, Part I

Viewing

As you lie embalmed,
our photo looks
out from the collage
across the room:
two boys in front
of a sunflower
twice their height.
You hold a jar
of fireflies—
muted in sunlight.

Trilogy 4

dreadlocks
falling out
she kisses my scar

in wilting leaves
one ripe tomato
the pickers missed

Christmas garden
we don't explain the silence
between our bodies

About the Author

Michael Morical studied East Asian Languages and Literatures at Indiana University. That led him to Taiwan, Japan and India where he taught English and wrote about life there. He studied poetry at the City College of New York with Marie Ponsot, Marilyn Hacker, Elaine Equi and other poets. Morical's work has appeared in *The New York Quarterly, Barrow Street, The Pedestal Magazine* and other journals. Finishing Line Press published *Sharing Solitaire*, his first chapbook, in 2008. He is currently a freelance writer in Taipei and an assistant editor of *The Same*.

TIMELESS
Trivia

Volume One

by

BOB HAMMITT

Edited by
CHRIS BANGS

FROM THE AUTHOR

Thank you for purchasing "Timeless Trivia Volume One!"

I've had an affinity for trivia my entire life. As a child, my family used to go on long road trips. We were forced to find ways to entertain each other, and my parents always thought that would be a good time to challenge our minds as well. So, everything from state capitals, to music, to world series winners, etc...became fair game in the back of that big old Chrysler.

As I got older and began to teach and coach, playing trivia was always something to do for fun during down times. When I would work at baseball camps, I'd always bring some starburst or some other prize for the kids during breaks or other spaces where appropriate.

When the Covid 19 virus caused us all to quarantine in the spring of 2020, some of my former students asked me to host a trivia game on Instagram live. So, we did that for about three months with 30-40 players participating each night. Most of the questions from this book are products of what we called "ronatrivia."

I tried to create questions for everyone from senior citizens to teenagers. Hopefully you will find some questions on topics that you are already knowledgable on, while others are in areas where you don't know much might be able to teach you a few things.

The best part of the "ronatrivia" was that it reconnected me with old friends and them with each other. We passed the time, had a few laughs, and learned a few things. Hopefully, all of that will apply to you and yours when you read this book and quiz yourself or others.

Good luck and have fun!

- Bob Hammitt

1. In what state were the first shots of the American Civil War fired?

2. Name the singer of the 1992 country hit "Achy Breaky Heart" who is also the father of the superstar entertainer once known as Hannah Montana.

3. Name the hit series which debuted on NBC in 2016 that includes present-day scenes as well as flashbacks involving the lives of the Pearson family.

4. What is the name of the mountain range which separates France and Spain?

5. Name the singer whose 2008-09 tour was the highest grossing by a female artist in history.

6. Of all NFL quarterbacks who have won two or more Super Bowls, which comes first alphabetically by last name?

7. In the movie and play "The Lion King," who is Simba's dad?

Answers

1) South Carolina
3) "This is Us"
5) Madonna
7.) Mufasa

2) Billy Ray Cyrus
4) Pyrenees
6) Troy Aikman

* 12 quarterbacks have won multiple Super Bowls: Ben Roethlisberger, Bart Starr, Roger Staubach, Bob Griese, Terry Bradshaw, Jim Plunkett, Joe Montana, Troy Aikman, John Elway, Tom Brady, Eli Manning, and Peyton Manning

8. In "Charlotte's Web," what type of animal is Wilbur?

9. On the "seventh day of Christmas," what kind of birds did "my true love" give to me?

10. On what state's license plates would one find the words "Live Free or Die?"

11. For which movie did Tom Hanks receive his first Academy Award nomination?

12. Name the country music singer who had a hit in 2011 with "Springsteen?"

13. Name the television show about a Jewish interior designer and a gay lawyer which stopped airing in 2006, then resumed airing in 2017.

14. Name the third book in the "Hunger Games" trilogy.

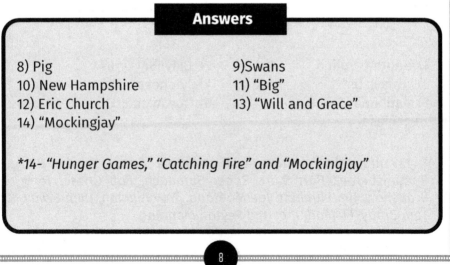

Answers

8) Pig   9)Swans
10) New Hampshire   11) "Big"
12) Eric Church   13) "Will and Grace"
14) "Mockingjay"

*14- "Hunger Games," "Catching Fire" and "Mockingjay"

15. Name the first ever non-European city to host the Olympics.

16. Who was the author of "The Tell Tale Heart" and "The Raven?"

17. In what year did the first moon landing, the Charles Manson murders, and Woodstock all take place?

18. Name the legendary rock band which visited the sketch "Wayne's World" on an episode of "Saturday Night Live" on February 17, 1990.

19. Who was the first President of the United States to be born in a hospital?

20. In the game of chess, with how many bishops does each player begin?

21. In a standard deck of cards, how many eyeballs are showing?

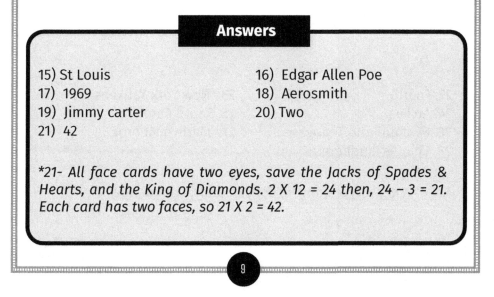

Answers

15) St Louis   16) Edgar Allen Poe
17) 1969   18) Aerosmith
19) Jimmy carter   20) Two
21) 42

21- All face cards have two eyes, save the Jacks of Spades & Hearts, and the King of Diamonds. 2 X 12 = 24 then, 24 − 3 = 21. Each card has two faces, so 21 X 2 = 42.

22. Which amendment to the United States Constitution protects Americans against "unreasonable searches and seizures?"

23. Which Major League Baseball team has won the most World Series?

24. Of Utah's five National Parks, which one comes first alphabetically?

25. Which state is nicknamed "The Palmetto State"?

26. Only two states share a border with eight other states. Name them.

27. Name the actress/model who was married to Arthur Miller and Joe DiMaggio.

28. Who was the first person to fly solo across the Atlantic Ocean?

Answers

22. Fourth   23. New York Yankees
24. Arches   25. South Carolina
26. Missouri and Tennessee   27. Marilyn Monroe
28. Charles Lindbergh

*24- *Arches, Bryce Canyon, Canyonlands, Capitol Reef, Zion*

29. Who was the first American president to serve only one term as president?

30. Name the 1991 film based on a 11-year-old character named Vada Sultenfuss which shares its title with a 1965 hit single by the Temptations.

31. Name the Jewish holiday which is also known as the "Day of Atonement."

32. Name the first single in the history of Billboard's Top 200 which reached No. 1 after the singer had died?

33. Name the singer whose hit singles include "Sign of the Times," "Watermelon Sugar," and "Adore You."

34. Who was the youngest person to win an American presidential election?

35. Which is the first element listed on the Periodic Table?

Answers

29) John Adams
31) Yom Kippur
33) Harry Styles
35) Hydrogen

30) "My Girl"
32) "(Sittin' on) the Dock of the Bay"
34) John F. Kennedy

32- Otis Redding died in a plane crash three days after recording his only No. 1 hit. He was going to come back to add the last verse of lyrics, that is why it is whistled.

36. In which state was the show "One Tree Hill" set?

37. Who was the most recent sitting U.S. president to be awarded the Nobel Peace Prize?

38. Which city is the capital of Idaho?

39. In 2003, "Fountains of Wayne" had a No. 1 hit with a song about whose mom?

40. In which animated television show does the theme song describe the main character as "absorbent and yellow and porous?"

41. Name the tennis player who was named the "Sports Illustrated Sportsman of the Year" in 1982.

42. According to the Church of Jesus Christ of Latter Day Saints, leader Joseph Smith found gold plates which he translated into the "Book of Mormon." In which American State did he find them?

Answers

36) North Carolina   37) Barack Obama
38) Boise   39) Stacy's
40) "Spongebob Squarepants" 41) Arthur Ashe
42) New York

37- Four presidents have won the Nobel Peace Prize: Theodore Roosevelt, Woodrow Wilson, Jimmy Carter and Barack Obama.

43. As of 2019, who is the oldest person ever to win a U.S. presidential election?

44. Where did quarterback Tom Brady play college football?

45. A book written by Delia Owens sold more than any other on Amazon in 2019. What was the title of that book?

46. Name the artist whose works graced the covers of 322 issues of "The Saturday Evening Post."

47. At 8 minutes and 36 seconds, what is the longest single ever to reach No. 1 on the billboard chart?

48. Name the famous building located at 1600 Pennsylvania Avenue.

49. Which insurance company started airing commercials in 2004 featuring the catchphrase "So easy a caveman could do it."?

Answers

43) Donald Trump   44) University of Michigan
45) "Where The Crawdads Sing"   46) Norman Rockwell
47) "American Pie"   48) The White House
49) Geico

43- Donald Trump was 70 years old when elected, Ronald Reagan was second oldest at 69 years old.

50. In the acronym SCUBA, what does the "C" stand for?

51. Name the famous magician who was born Erich Weisz on March 24, 1874, in Budapest, Hungary.

52. The very first _____ club was founded in Salem, Oregon, in 1929.

53. Name the television show that set a record by winning its 5th straight Emmy award for best comedy in 1998.

54. Which U.S. president famously said, "the only thing we have to fear is fear itself," in his inaugural address?

55. Name the series of short animated films from the 1940s based upon the love/hate relationship between a cat and a mouse.

56. In the Presidential election of 1960, who was the Republican nominee defeated by John F. Kennedy?

Answers

50) Contained
52) Mickey Mouse
54) Franklin D. Roosevelt
56) Richard Nixon

51) Harry Houdini
53)"Frasier"
55)"Tom and Jerry"

50- S.C.U.B.A. stands for "Self-Contained Underwater Breathing Apparatus"

57. In 1999, Charles Barkley played in his final NBA game for which team?

58. Name the linebacker who is the only NFL hall-of-famer to attend Baylor University.

59. Which city is the capital of South Korea?

60. What was the name of Forrest Gump's "shrimpin' boat?"

61. In the quadratic formula, was it the denominator?

62. Name the director of the 1994 film, "Pulp Fiction."

63. With just over 17,000 words, which is Shakespeare's shortest tragedy?

Answers

57) Houston Rockets

58) Mike Singletary

59) Seoul

60) Jenny

61) 2A

62) Quintin Tarantino

63) "Macbeth"

64. Name the boy band who released its debut album in 2011 titled "Up All Night."

65. Which team has made the most appearances in the NBA finals?

66. How many black keys are there on a piano?

67. In the pilot episode of "The Office," which employee was in their first day on the job?

68. Name the only continent on which one would not be able to find bees.

69. Name the former governor of Alabama who once famously demanded "segregation today, segregation tomorrow, segregation forever."

70. Name the only major league baseball team to be named after a snake.

Answers

64) One Direction
66) 36
68) Antarctica
70) Arizona Diamondbacks

65) Lakers
67) Ryan Howard
69) George Wallace

As of 2020, the Lakers have appeared 31 times, the Celtics 21 times, and the 76ers are third with nine appearances.

71. Name the famous rapper who's birth name was Calvin Broadus.

72. What is the scientific name for a group of kittens?

73. Which state did former civil rights activist John Lewis represent in the United States Congress until his death in 2020?

74. Of all the cities in the world that can be spelled in five letters or less, which is the most populated?

75. What is the proper name for an angle which is more than 90 degrees, but less than 180 degrees?

76. Who is the NBA's career assists leader?

77. Name the hip hop group whose 1996 debut album was titled "The Score."

Answers

71) Snoop Dogg   72) A Kindle
73) Georgia   74) Tokyo
75) Obtuse   76) John Stockton
77) The Fugees

74- Delhi, India, is the second most populated city spelled in five letters.

78. What is the third most populous American city?

79. Name the rock group who performed for the first time In the United States on February 11, 1964, in Washington, D.C.

80. This model of shoe was named after a basketball coach in 1921. In the United States today, a pair is sold every 43 seconds. Name that model of shoe.

81. Who is the only person ever to win two unshared Nobel prizes?

82. What number is represented by the Roman numeral sequence LXIV ?

83. Fill in the blank from the popular song "Tiny Dancer" by Elton John: "Pretty eyed, pirate smile, you'll marry a _____ man."

84. Which group won the "record of the year" Grammy in 2004 with "Clocks?"

Answers

78) Chicago
80) Chuck Taylor
82) 64
84) Coldplay

79) The Beatles
81) Linus Pauling
83) Music

81- In 1954, Pauling was awarded the Nobel Prize for Chemistry, and in 1962, he won the Nobel Peace Prize.

85. By what name is Samuel Langhorne Clemens better known?

86. Name the comedian that wrote, produced, and starred in the 1998 movie "Half Baked."

87. Name the first freshman to ever win college football's Heisman Trophy?

88. Name the epic British poem set in 6th century Scandinavia about a hero who travels great distances to prove his strength at impossible odds against supernatural demons and beasts.

89. Who was the first woman ever to win an Oscar, Grammy, Emmy, Peabody, and Golden Globe award?

90. In the acronym "R.A.D.A.R.," what does the "D" stand for?

91. The longhorn is the official animal of which state?

Answers

85. Mark Twain

86. Dave Chappelle

87. Johnny Manziel

88. "Beowulf"

89. Barbara Streisand

90. Detection

91. Texas

90- R.A.D.A.R. stands for "Radio Detection and Ranging"

92. Which planet is closest to the sun?

93. Name the musical term which in Italian means "growing," and means to gradually play louder.

94. Name the very large tree which is seven letters long and contains all five vowels.

95. Name the 1962 hit by Bobby Pickett which featured the line, "The coffin bangers were about to arrive with their vocal group The Crypt-Kicker Five."

96. Name the rapper whose hits include "Miami." "Jiggy Wit It," and "Summertime."

97. What is the nickname of the annual college football game between the University of Alabama and Auburn University?

98. Name the doctor who in 1956 announced that he had successfully tested the first vaccine for polio.

Answers

92. Mercury
94. Sequoia
96. Will Smith
98. Jonas Salk

93. Crescendo
95. "The Monster Mash"
97. The Iron Bowl

99. Who is the only U.S. president who also served on the U.S. Supreme Court?

100. In which American city was the hit television show "Cheers" set?

101. Give the one word title of the 1984 film about Wolfgang Mozart, which was also his middle name.

102. Name the former U.S. president and war hero whose picture is on the $50 bill.

103. In 2002, Johnny Cash released the single "Hurt." Name the band who originally recorded this song.

104. S.I.M. as in "Sim Card" is an acronym. What does the "I" stand for?

105. Name the 1985 film about a group of adolescents and their quest to find the treasure of One Eyed Willie.

Answers

99) William Howard Taft
101) "Amadeus"
103) Nine Inch Nails
105) "The Goonies"

100) Boston
102) Ulysses S. Grant
104) Identity

104- S.I.M. stands for "Subscriber Identity Module"

106. *Rolling Stone* magazine said her hit titled "Thank You......Next" was the seventh best song of the 2010's. Name her.

107. Name the actor who starred in the movies "Elf" and "Honeymoon in Vegas," born March 26, 1940 in the Bronx.

108. What are the rights that law enforcement officers are required to read to someone who is being placed under arrest most commonly named?

109. In which year did Major League Baseball not have a World Series because of player's strike?

110. Who was the first female ever to serve on the U.S. Supreme Court?

111. What is the last name of the person who became Canada's 23rd Prime Minister in 2015?

112. Name the Netflix series which debuted in 2017 based upon a series of audio tapes detailing the reasoning behind a teenager's suicide.

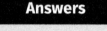

Answers

106) Ariana Grande
108) Miranda Rights
110) Sandra Day O'Conner
112) "Thirteen Reasons Why"

107) James Caan
109) 1994
111) Trudeau

111- Justin Trudeau's father, Pierre Trudeau, served as Prime Minister of Canada from 1980-1984

113. Name the dramatic teen drama series on HBO which debuted in 2019 and is based on an Israeli show by the same name.

114. What is the lowest number which when spelled contains the letter "A?"

115. In what year did the United States drop atomic bombs on Hiroshima and Nagasaki, Japan?

116. Name the 1974 film starring Burt Reynolds as Paul Crewe, which was remade in 2005 with Adam Sandler playing the same role.

117. Who has more total wins than any other pitcher in Major League Baseball history?

118. Name the actor who starred as Kevin Arnold in the television series "The Wonder Years."

119. In 1992, an NBA playoff game between the Portland Trail Blazers and the Los Angeles Lakers was moved 300 miles due to the L.A. riots. Name the university which hosted this game.

Answers

113. "Euphoria"   114. One Thousand
115. 1945   116. "The Longest Yard"
117. Cy Young   118. Fred Savage
119. University of Nevada Las Vegas

117- With 511 wins, Cy Young is baseball's all-time win leader, and with 315 losses, he also leads in that category.

120. Three of the ten highest waterfalls in America are located in one national park. Name it.

121. In the 1980's, which fast food restaurant regularly used the phrase "Where's the Beef?" in its commercials?

122. Name the 2005 film directed by Ron Howard starring Russell Crowe about the life of depression era boxer James Braddock.

123. Name the country music singer born in 1955 in Oklahoma who was once named country music's female artist of the year four times in a row and whose hits include "Is There Life Out There?" and "Does He Love You?"

124. Name the western-most state which does not observe daylight savings time.

125. Name the longest running animated show in American television history.

126. What is the minimum number of electoral college votes needed to win the U.S. presidential election?

Answers

120) Yosemite
122) Cinderella Man
124) Hawaii
126) 270

121) Wendy's
123) Reba McEntire
125) The Simpsons

124- Only two states do not observe daylight savings time: Hawaii and Arizona

127. What is the first name of the "Game of Thrones" character who is also known as "The Kingslayer?"

128. Which animal is on the logo of the Porsche automobile logo?

129. Name the university which Lovell Edwards led to a national college football championship in 1984.

130. In the movie "Mean Girls" on what day of the week do a group of girls known as "the plastics" wear pink?

131. What is the more common pen name of Theodore Geisel, who also published propaganda for the United States during World War Two?

132. In which state would you find Theodore Roosevelt National Park?

133. Name the only running back to rush for 2000 yards in a season of college football and 2000 yards in a season in the National Football League.

Answers

127) Jamie
129) Brigham Young University
131) Dr. Seuss
133) Barry Sanders

128) Horse
130) Wednesday
132) North Dakota

133- There are seven players who have rushed for 2000 yards in an NFL season, and 26 have done it in Division One college football. Sanders is the only athlete on both lists.

134. Stanley Burrell was once the batboy for the Oakland Athletics. When he grew up he became a popular musician performing under a different name. What was that name?

135. Name the musical that was inspired by the life of Maria Von Trapp.

136. Which two states are connected by the Tillman-O'Callaghan Bridge?

137. What is the name of the unit, approximately six feet long, used to measure the depth of water?

138. Name the Australian singer whose hits include "Riptide," "Saturday Sun," and "Mess is Mine."

139. Of the twelve disciples of Jesus, which one comes last alphabetically?

140. Which organization has won the most NHL championships?

Answers

134) M.C. Hammer
135) "The Sound of Music"
136) Arizona and Nevada
137) Fathom
138) Vance Joy
139) Thomas
140) Montreal Canadiens

* Players thought Stanley looked like Hank Aaron, whose nickname was "the hammer," so they began calling him "lil' hammer."

141. On her 2011 hit "Blaze of Glory," who backed Lady Gaga on saxophone?

142. On the hit NBC comedy "Parks and Recreation," what is the name of the musical alter ego of Ron Swanson?

143. The 1992 U.S. men's Olympic basketball team is often referred to as "The Dream Team." Who was the only amateur player on that team?

144. What is the most populous country in Africa?

145. In darts, what is the highest score possible to achieve by throwing three darts?

146. In what city is the popular board game "Monopoly" set?

147. In sheet music, how many beats does a whole note receive?

Answers

141) Clarence Clemons   142) Duke Silver
143) Christian Laetner   144) Nigeria
145) 180   146) Atlantic City
147) Four

*141- Clemons, who was the longtime saxophonist in Bruce Springsteen's E Street Band, died just a few weeks after recording with Lady Gaga.

148. London hosted the first summer Olympics held after World War Two in 1948. Name the city which hosted the previous summer games, and the year it was hosted.

149. After World War Two, a group started sending boxed necessities to war-torn Europe. They were called the Cooperative for American Remittance. When similar type shipments are sent today, what do we usually call them?

150. Only one city in America has hosted the Winter Olympics twice. Which state is that city in?

151. In the 1994 film "Dumb and Dumber," what was Lloyd's last name?

152. Name the first month of the year which does not contain the letter "A."

153. In water polo, how many players are there on each side?

154. Name the only mammal that scientists believe to be incapable of tasting sweetness.

Answers

148) Berlin, Germany 1936   149) C.A.R.E. packages
150) New York   151) Christmas
152) June   153) Seven
154) Cats

150- Lake Placid, New York, hosted the winter Olympics in 1932 and 1980.

155. The song "Hallelujah" had been recorded by over 300 artists. Name the late singer/songwriter who wrote it in 1984.

156. Name the rock star who was a former teacher and got his stage name because of a black and yellow sweater he used to regularly wear on stage early in his career.

157. Who is the only NBA player ever to score 100 points in a single game?

158. In which Midwestern city did rapper Eminem grow up?

159. Name the innovation added into the NBA for the 1979 season.

160. Eric Clapton wrote the rock classic "Layla" about another musicians wife. Name that musician.

161. Near the end of the movie "The Sandlot," the boys go to the home of the dog they have referred to as "the beast." It is there that they find out that the dog's real name is _____.

Answers

155) Leonard Cohen
157) Wilt Chamberlain
159) Three point line
161) Hercules

156) Sting
158) Detroit
160) George Harrison

160- "Layla" and "Wonderful Tonight" were both written about model Pattie Boyd, who divorced Harrison and married Clapton.

162. What is the title of the 1984 film starring Prince, which also featured a soundtrack that was the top selling album of that year?

163. In what city is the movie "Spiderman" based?

164. In 2015, alt country rocker Ryan Adams covered an entire Taylor Swift album. What is the name of that album?

165. Which former president of the United States was the target of two assassination attempts in a 17-day period?

166. What is the lowest number that when spelled, the letters go in alphabetical order?

167. In math, what is the fraction 22/7 better known as?

168. In what state was the transcontinental railroad completed?

Answers

162) "Purple Rain"
164) 1989
166) Forty
168) Utah

163) New York
165) Gerald Ford
167) Pi

165- The second attempt to assassinate President Ford, on September 5, 1975, was by Manson family member Lynette "Squeaky" Fromme.

169. In the television series "Gilligan's Island," what is the name of the shipwrecked boat?

170. Which beer company began airing commercials in 2017 which featured the phrase "dilly dilly?"

171. Name the artist who won the 2020 song of the year for her hit "Bad Guy."

172. This famous landmark opened in 1889. Standing at 984 feet, it was the tallest building in the world at the time. Name it.

173. Name the host of the television show, "Lifestyles of the Rich and Famous," who would sign off each show wishing the viewers, "Champagne wishes and caviar dreams."

174. Name the only country not to win a single gold medal at the summer Olympics while they hosted them.

175. Who was the Democratic nominee for president in the 2000 election?

Answers

169) S.S. Minnow
170) Bud Light
171) Billie Eilish
172) Eiffel Tower
173) Robin Leach
174) Canada
175) Al Gore

169: The "Minnow" was named after F.C.C. director Newton Minnow, who is noted for a 1961 speech in which he called television a "vast wasteland."

176. Name the major newspaper that has used the slogan "All the News That's Fit To Print" since 1897.

177. Name the civil rights leader who was born in 1927, who led and organized agricultural workers to band together to fight for their rights, and who founded the National Farm Workers Association.

178. In 1981, President Ronald Reagan was shot by John Hinkley, Jr. Name the actress Hinkley later confessed that he was trying to impress.

179. In the "Twilight" series of books and movies, what state does Bella move to Washington from?

180. How many states begin with the word "New?"

181. Name the successful children's author whose books include "Runaway Ralph," "Ramona Quimby: Age 8," and "Henry Huggins."

182. In the movie "Airplane," which dish causes passengers to become ill?

Answers

176). The New York Times   177) Caesar Chavez
178) Jodie Foster   179) Arizona
180) Four   181) Beverly Cleary
182) Fish

*180- New Jersey, New Mexico, New Hampshire, New York

183. Name the 2009 novel which was made into a feature film in 2011 based upon the relationship between a white journalist and black maids in Jackson, Mississippi.

184. On which television network did "Gossip Girl" air from 2007 to 2012?

185. Ivan Pavlov was a famed psychologist because of his theories on conditioned response. What type of animal did he mainly use for his studies?

186. Adirondack State Park is the largest state park of which state?

187. This country music legend was inspired to become a musician while watching Johnny Cash play a concert at San Quentin prison. Name him.

188. What popular toy company gets its name from the Danish expression "play well."

189. "Wings" served as the back-up band for which former member of the Beatles?

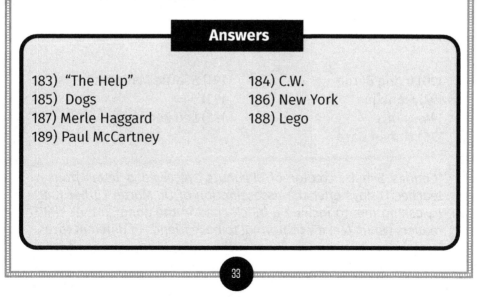

Answers

183) "The Help"   184) C.W.
185) Dogs   186) New York
187) Merle Haggard   188) Lego
189) Paul McCartney

190. Name the Jewish refugee to America who wrote both "White Christmas' and "God Bless America."

191. Who is the only Major League Baseball team never to appear in a World Series?

192. The comic strip "Peanuts" introduced an African American character after the assassination of Martin Luther King Jr. Name that character.

193. Other than one, what is the smallest number that is both a square number and a cubed number?

194. The Statue of Liberty was a gift from which country?

195. Name the classic rock band whose drummer drowned on his own vomit in 1980, causing the band to cease recording together.

196. Name the legendary Motown singer who was shot and killed by his own father April 1, 1984.

Answers

190) Irving Berlin
192) Franklin
194) France
196) Marvin Gaye

191) Seattle Mariners
193) 64
195) Led Zeppelin

Charles Schulz, creator of "Peanuts," received a letter from a teacher 11 days after the assassination of Dr. Martin Luther King Jr., asking him to include a black child in the gang so that child readers would feel it was normal to have friends of different races.

197. H.G.H. stands for "Human Growth Hormone." Which gland in the human body produces it?

198. When Theodore Roosevelt gave his inaugural address in 1905, he was the only president to ever do so without using what word?

199. Name the theater in which Abraham Lincoln was murdered.

200. In terms of square miles, what is the second largest country in the world?

201. He was born Brian Hugh Warner, but as a singer he is known by the combination of two cultural icons: an actress and a serial killer. What is that name by which he is famous?

202. Name the Netflix series which premiered in 2015 and chronicles the story of cartels and drug kingpins in the late 1980s.

203. Who was the first person ever inducted into the Basketball Hall of Fame as both a player and a coach?

Answers

197) Pituitary   198) "I"
199) Ford's Theater   200) Canada
201) Marilyn Manson   202) "Narcos"
203) John Wooden

*201 "Marilyn Manson" is the combination of Marilyn Monroe and Charles Manson.

204. Name the female singer and rapper whose songs include "Good as Hell," "Truth Hurts," and "Juice."

205. What does the prefix "hemi" mean?

206. What body of water is touched by the nations of Saudi Arabia, Iraq, Iran and Kuwait?

207. Name the actor and comedian who also plays the banjo and has won a Grammy for best bluegrass album.

208. Name the legendary grunge band that once was called "Mookie Blaylock."

209. Which NFL team has appeared in the most Super Bowls?

210. In 2018, Gary Oldman won the Academy award for Best Actor for his portrayal of which historical figure in the film "Darkest Hour?"

Answers

204) Lizzo
206) Persian Gulf
208) Pearl Jam
210) Winston Churchill

205) Half
207) Steve Martin
209) New England Patriots

The name "Pearl Jam" comes from lead singer Eddie Vedder's great grandmother, Pearl. He has said that she was a Native American who used to make toast with a peyote-laced spread on top.

211. Who, in 1994 at the age of 45, became the oldest man ever to become heavyweight champion of the boxing world?

212. In Lacrosse, how many players are there on each side?

213. Of all of the United States which touch the Pacific Ocean, which comes first alphabetically?

214. The 2001 movie "Super Troopers" is based on five highway patrolmen from which state?

215. Which NFL team did video game icon John Madden once lead to a Super Bowl victory?

216. When you list the first names of the Spice Girls alphabetically, which comes last?

217. Which professional sports team got its name because of its fans being forced to avoid being hit by trolleys?

Answers

211) George Foreman
213) Alaska
215) Oakland Raiders
217) Dodgers

212) 10
214) Vermont
216) Sporty

216- The Spice Girls are comprised of Scary, Sporty, Baby, Ginger and Posh

218. According to the Old Testament of the Bible, who is the father of both Isaac and Ishmael?

219. What is the tallest peak in the continental United States?

220. As of 2020, which NCAA basketball team has made more appearances in the "Sweet Sixteen" than any other?

221. With nearly 12 million visitors in 2019, which National Park had more visitors than any other?

222. Name the artist who painted "The Starry Night," "The Potato Eaters," and "The Yellow House."

223. For which University did Dwayne "The Rock" Johnson play college football?

224. The 2015 movie "Straight Outta Compton" was about the rise and fall of which rap group?

Answers

21). Abraham
220) University of Kentucky

219) Mt. Whitney
221) Great Smoky Mountain National Park

222) Vincent Van Gogh
223) University of Miami

224) N.W.A.

As of 2020, the schools with the most appearances in the sweet sixteen are the University of Kentucky (43), University of North Carolina (33), U.C.L.A. (33), University of Kansas (31)

225. Which Major League Baseball team features "sausage races" before the bottom of the sixth inning of each home game?

226. Name the singer whose albums include "Lust For Life," "Ultraviolence," and "Born to Die."

227. Name the comedian and actor who was born October 31, 1950, and died on March 4, 1994. Hint: his date of birth is quite ironic when you consider his last name.

228. In which state is the annual musical festival known as "Coachella" held?

229. Name the American playwright whose works include "The Odd Couple," "Promises, Promises," and "Brighton Beach Memoirs."

230. *Quartz Magazine* calls this miniseries about a nuclear accident in the Soviet Union the best miniseries of all time. Name it.

231. What does the "T" in "S.W.A.T." stand for?

Answers

225) Milwaukie Brewers   226) Lana Del Ray
227). John Candy   228) California
229) Neil Simon   230)"Chernobyl"
231) Tactics

* 231- S.W.A.T. stands for "Special Weapons and Tactics"

232. Who wrote the play "Hamilton" and starred as the title character?

233. Of the 50 United States capitals, which one is located furthest south?

234. Name the contemporary pop star who has released three albums using math symbols as their titles.

235. For all of his box office success in hugely popular films, Harrison Ford has only been nominated for an Academy Award one time. For what film was he nominated?

236. Name the Confederate Civil War General whose house overlooks Arlington National Cemetery.

237. Whose album titled "Scorpion" was rated the tenth best of the year 2018 by *Rolling Stone Magazine*?

238. Name the author who wrote "Jurassic Park."

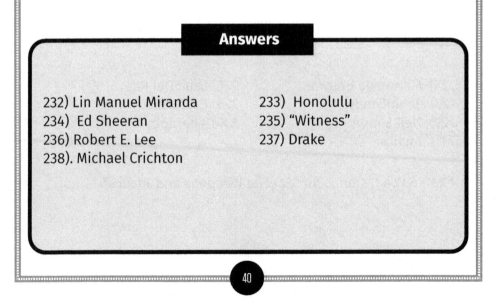

Answers

232) Lin Manuel Miranda
234) Ed Sheeran
236) Robert E. Lee
238). Michael Crichton

233) Honolulu
235) "Witness"
237) Drake

239. Name the creature that is considered the largest mammal in the ocean.

240. Name the city in Spain which hosts the "Running of the Bulls" each year.

241. Name the Mexican food which, in Spanish, means "little donkey."

242. Name the Daft Punk song which won the Grammy for Record of the Year in 2014.

243. Name the former Saturday Night Live cast member who went on to star in many movies, including "Beverly Hills Cop," "Coming to America," and "The Nutty Professor."

244. Who is the only athlete to play in both a Super Bowl and a World Series?

245. What Is the name of the company which manufactures agricultural, forestry, and construction equipment and is based in Moline, Illinois?

Answers

239) Blue Whale
241). Burrito
243) Eddie Murphy
245) John Deere

240) Pamplona
242) "Get Lucky"
244) Deion Sanders

244- Sanders appeared in the World Series with the Atlanta Braves, and won Super Bowls as a San Francisco 49er and Dallas Cowboy

246. Kanye West released an album in 2016 titled "Life of _____."

247. Name the pop singer who got married on New Year's Eve of 2004, a marriage which lasted only 55 hours.

248. In which state is the largest shopping mall in the United States?

249. In 1936, Bruno Hauptman was executed for the murder of which celebrity's child?

250. In the 1985 movie "The Breakfast Club," what is the first name of the character portrayed by Molly Ringwald?

251. In his first four balls, a bowler knocks down 6 pins with their first throw; 4 with their second; 9 with their third; and one with their fourth. What is their score at the end of the first frame?

252. The Iran-Contra scandal occurred during which President's second term?

Answers

246) Pablo
248) Minnesota
250) Claire
252) Ronald Reagan

247) Brittney Spears
249) Charles Lindbergh
251) 19

*248- The "Mall of America" has more than 500 stores and is located in Bloomington, Minnesota

253. Name the winner of the 2013 Academy Award for best picture, which was directed Ben Affleck.

254. Which college football team plays its home games in a stadium nicknamed "The Big House?"

255. First performed on Christmas Eve of 1818, this is considered the most played Christmas song of all time. Name it.

256. Which famous magazine published its first issue in 1953 with a picture of Lucille Ball and her newborn son on the cover.

257. Name the rap group that released the album "License to Ill" in 1986.

258. What is the name of the British anthropologist who wrote the book "My Life With Chimpanzees."

259. During an episode in the 8th season of Seinfeld, Kramer lost sleep because of a bright blinking sign. That sign was a part of which restaurant?

Answers

253) Argo
255) Silent Night
257) Beastie Boys
259) Kenny Rogers Roasters

254) University of Michigan
256) T.V. Guide
258) Jane Goodale

260. T.E.D. talks are very popular in the 21st century. What does "T.E.D." stand for?

261. In which state is the animated television show "Family Guy" set?

262. Name the type of poem that consists of 14 lines, with each line consisting of ten syllables. Shakespeare wrote 154 of them.

263. Of all the players in Major League Baseball history whose last name begins with T, which one hit the most home runs?

264. Name the scientist whose third law states, "For every action, there is an equal and opposite reaction."

265. Name the 2004 movie about a teen wishing she was older, and suddenly finding herself in her third decade of life.

266. Yorba Linda, California, is home to which president's presidential library?

Answers

260) Technology, entertainment, design 261) Rhode Island
262) Sonnet   263) Jim Thome
264) Isaac Newton   265) Thirteen Going on Thirty
266) Richard Nixon

263- Jim Thome hit 612 career home runs, Frank Thomas is second with 521.

267. In Greek mythology, who is the god of the sea?

268. Name the band whose 1979 album titled "Breakfast in America" included the hit singles "Take the Long Way Home," "Goodbye Stranger," and "The Logical Song."

269. According to *Billboard Magazine*, which artist had the top two singles of 2016.

270. 15 of the 19 hijackers who executed the September, 11, 2001, terrorist attacks were from the same country. Which country?

271. In what 1992 Disney animated film did Robin Williams voice-act the role of Genie?

272. Of the 50 United States, which has the most counties?

273. When you list all the events that comprise the decathlon alphabetically, which comes last?

Answers

267) Poseiden
269) Justin Beiber
271) "Aladdin"
273) Shot put

268) Supertramp
270) Saudi Arabia
272) Texas

273- The events of the decathlon are pole vault, high jump, long jump, shot put, discus, 100 meters, 400 meters, 1500 meters, javelin, 110 meter hurdles

274. Which month features a day in which the convenience store chain, 711, gives away free Slurpees?

275. In the movie "Ted 2," from which NFL quarterback did Ted and John try to steal?

276. Whitney Houston's No. 1 hit "I Will Always Love You" was on the soundtrack of what movie, which also starred her?

277. Who was the first secretary of the treasury in the history of the United States?

278. What interstate goes through Spokane and Minneapolis on the way to Chicago?

279. Which human organ cleans approximately 50 gallons of blood every day?

280. In the 1977 film "Smokey and the Bandit," what brand of beer is the Bandit trying to transport from Atlanta to Texarkana?

Answers

274) July

275) Tom Brady

276) "The Bodyguard"

277) Alexander Hamilton

278) Interstate 90

279) Liver

280) Coors

280- Until 1976, Coors beer was only available in 11 states because it wasn't pasteurized.

281. How many laps comprise the Indianapolis 500?

282. Which college football team has a children's hospital overlooking the playing field, to which fans wave at the end of every first quarter?

283. This service and charity club was begun by businessmen in Detroit in 1915. Its name comes from a native American expression which means, "we share our talents." Name it.

284. Prior to becoming president of the United States, which state did Barack Obama represent in the United States Senate?

285. If you landed at George H.W. Bush International Airport, what city would you be in?

286. In the Homestead Act of 1862, how many acres of land were settlers awarded?

287. What is the most populous country in South America?

Answers

281) 200
283) Kiwanis
285) Houston
287) Brazil

282) University of Iowa
284) Illinois
286) 160

281- Each lap around the track is 2.5 miles long.

288. In which American national park would you find Jenny, Holly, and String Lakes?

289. Rob Pilatus and Fabrice Morvan paired to form what musical group in the late 1980s?

290. If the opposite and adjacent sides of a triangle are 12 inches and 5 inches respectively, how long is the hypotenuse?

291. Which Major League Baseball stadium has the greatest seating capacity?

292. In which state was the television show "Glee" set?

293. Name the famous poet and author who turned 40 the same day her friend, Dr. Martin Luther King, Jr., was assassinated.

294. Which of the four oceans contain the most coral reefs?

Answers

288) Grand Teton National Park 289) Milli Vanilli
290) 13 inches   291) Dodger Stadium
292) Ohio   293) Maya Angelou
294) Pacific

291- The stadiums with the highest seating capacity are Dodger Stadium (56,000), Yankee Stadium (53,325), Coors Field (49,469) and Chase Field (48, 663)

295. In the card game cribbage, how many points is three of a kind worth?

296. Name the American folk icon who wrote "This Land is Your land."

297. Only two states do not have self-service gasoline across their state. Which ones?

298. Who replaced Paul Hackett as the head football coach at the University of Southern California in 2000?

299. In 2019, which artist became the first female to win the Grammy for best rap album?

300. What do the initials of the fashion brand D.K.N.Y. stand for?

301. In terms of square miles, which is the largest Canadian Province?

Answers

295) 6
296) Woody Guthrie
297) New Jersey and Oregon
298) Pete Carroll
299) Cardi B
300) Don't Knock New York
301) Quebec

302. What is the proper name for a group of dolphins?

303. On the television sitcom "Married With Children," what was Al Bundy's wife's first name?

304. Name the poet who is often called the father of American Free Verse, whose most famous works include "Song of Myself" and "I Sing the Body Electric."

305. Which soap opera has won more daytime Emmys than any other?

306. In August, 1959, what became America's 50th state?

307. In 2008, who became the oldest pitcher to ever start a World Series game?

308. Name the city in which the Wizard of Oz lived.

Answers

302) A pod
304) Walt Whitman
306) Hawaii
308) Emerald City

303) Peggy
305) "The Young and the Restless"
307) Jamie Moyer

In 2012, Moyer became the oldest pitcher in regular season history to win a game at age 49 for the Colorado Rockies.

309. Name the 1950's novel featuring the character Holden Caulfield.

310. Name the actor who played the character Troy Bolton in "High School Musical."

311. The word "vaccine" comes from the Spanish word for which animal?

312. In the abbreviation P.M., as in time of day, what does the P stand for?

313. In which state did the surrender of General Lee to General Grant happen, ending the American Civil War?

314. Prior to the eruption of Mt. St Helens in 1980, this was the last mountain in the continental United States to have an eruption, which was in 1915. Name it.

315. What is the nickname of the only NHL team to play its home games in the state of Missouri?

Answers

309) "The Catcher in the Rye" 310) Zach Efron
311) Cow 312) Post
313) Virginia 314) Mt. Lassen
315) Blues

316. Which Marvel production was the highest grossing film of 2019?

317. What would your zodiac sign be if you were born on the same date as a movie starring Tom Cruise about the struggles of a badly wounded Vietnam Veteran?

318. The Bible was the best selling book in America in the 19th century. What was the second-best selling book?

319. Three spiders are standing next to three crickets. How many legs are there?

320. In which European city is the Acropolis?

321. Name college football's all-time passing yardage leader by a quarterback.

322. Give the blood type whose hosts are often referred to as "universal donors."

Answers

316) "Black Panther"
318) "Uncle Tom's Cabin"
320) Athens
322) O negative

317) Cancer
319) 42
321) Drew Brees

*317- Cruise starred in the 1989 movie "Born on the Fourth of July," based on the autobiography of Vietnam war veteran Ron Kovic.

323. What is the name of the world famous artist who was born in Andalucia, Spain, in 1881?

324. Who was the first golfer to win $100,000 in prize money in one year?

325. The Olympic sport of curling is played with what common household cleaning item?

326. Name the only state capital that begins with the letter "N."

327. Which was the only Major League Baseball team to win two World Series championships in the 1980's?

328. Name the singer who suffered much criticism when she was caught lip syncing her hit single "Autobiography" on October 24, 2004.

329. A homonym for this food means "two." Name that food.

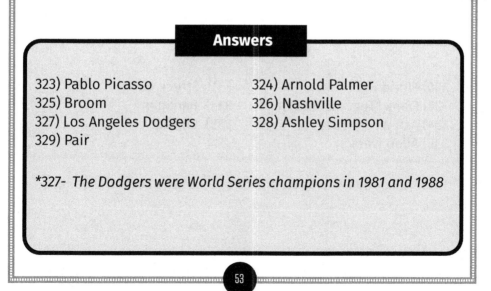

Answers

323) Pablo Picasso   324) Arnold Palmer
325) Broom   326) Nashville
327) Los Angeles Dodgers   328) Ashley Simpson
329) Pair

327- The Dodgers were World Series champions in 1981 and 1988

330. In what state would you find Cape Canaveral?

331. If a baseball player has a hat trick, it means he did what three times?

332. What is the first name of country music singer Tim McGraw's father, who recorded the final out on the mound for the 1980 world champion Philadelphia Phillies?

333. 4011 is the produce code at the grocery store for what fruit?

334. On what day of the week does the Catholic celebration known as Lent begin?

335. In 1970, this band named after a city had one of their biggest hits with a song that had three numbers in the title. Name the band.

336. In the first decade of this century, Kobe Bryant scored more points than any other player in the NBA. Who was the second leading scorer of that time period?

Answers

330) Florida
332) Frank "Tug" McGraw, Jr.
334) Ash Wednesday
336) Allen Iverson

331) Struck out
333) Bananas
335) Chicago

335- "25 or 6 to 4" was recorded for Chicago's second album.

337. Name the only president in American history who also won a Rhodes Scholarship.

338. With which NBA team did Michael Jordan play his final game?

339. Name the 2003 Disney movie about a timid clownfish father who must travel to Sydney, Australia, to find his son.

340. When the United States women's soccer team won the world cup in 1999, which country did it defeat?

341. Who is the only president in the history of the United States to serve two non-consecutive terms?

342. There are two letters that are the first letter of eight different states. One of them is N, as in Nevada. What is the other letter that 8 states start with?

343. He was born Chancelor Johnathan Bennett and he won the 2017 Grammy for best new artist. What is his stage name?

Answers

337) Bill Clinton

338) The Washington Wizards

339) "Finding Nemo"

340) China

341) Grover Cleveland

342) M

343) Chance the Rapper

Grover Cleveland won the election of 1884, then lost the election of 1888, even though he won the popular vote. He ran again in 1892 and won.

344. In what city is the headquarters to the United Nations located?

345. Name the brand of beer that features the number 33 on its label.

346. Which NFL running back had the most total yards rushing for the 1980's?

347. What state did 2008 Republican presidential candidate Mitt Romney serve as governor of from 2003 to 2007?

348. Name the R & B group that had two top ten singles in 1990 with "Poison" and "Do Me."

349. The first ever BCS championship game was played on January 4, 1999. Which university won that game?

350. What type of car did Marty McFly use to go back in time in the movie "Back to the Future?"

Answers

344) New York, New York
345) Rolling Rock
346) Eric Dickerson
347) Massachusetts
348) Bel Biv Devoe
349) University of Tennessee
350) DeLorean

349- The University of Tennessee defeated Florida State University 23-16 in the first B.C.S. title game.

351. Dr. James Naismith is credited with inventing what sport in 1891?

352. Which is the only U.S. state that grows coffee beans?

353. Which is the only dwarf in "Snow White and the Seven Dwarfs" whose name is not an adjective?

354. On the television show "Friends," what is the last name of the character played by Matthew Perry?

355. What color is Dora the Explorer's talking backpack?

356. Name the actor who played the role of Derek Zoolander in the 2001 movie: "Zoolander?"

357. "The Phantom of the Opera" is the longest running show on Broadway. What is the second-longest running show on Broadway?

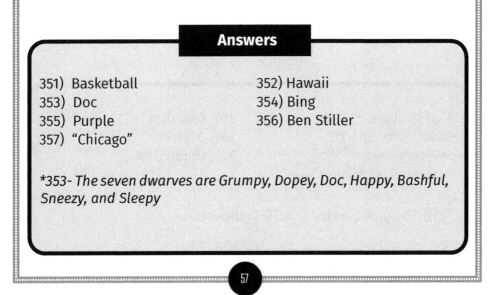

Answers

351) Basketball
353) Doc
355) Purple
357) "Chicago"

352) Hawaii
354) Bing
356) Ben Stiller

353- The seven dwarves are Grumpy, Dopey, Doc, Happy, Bashful, Sneezy, and Sleepy

358. If you drive at a rate of 45 miles per hour, how far would you travel in 20 minutes?

359. Name the popular 80s band whose hits included "Working for the Weekend," "Turn Me Loose," and "The Kid is Hot Tonight."

360. Name the 1999 movie starring Jennifer Aniston and Ron Livingston about white collar workers who hate their boss and decide to rebel against him.

361. What major rule change did the NFL make in 1974, which was first used in a regular season game on September 22nd 1974, between the Broncos and Steelers?

362. In the Bachman Tuner Overdrive song "Taking Care of Business," what time do you take the train into the city?

363. Gary Puckett had hits with the songs "Young Girl," "Lady Willpower," and "Over You." What was his backup band called?

364. Which president famously sent ping pong players to China as part of his "Détente" program?

Answers

358) 15 miles

360) "Office Space"

362) 8:15

364) Richard Nixon

359) Loverboy

361) Overtime

363) Union Gap

361- The game ended in a 35-35 draw.

365. What fictional city in Indiana was the NBC comedy "Parks and Recreation" set in?

366. What was the first sports-based movie to win the Academy Award for best picture?

367. Name the H.B.O. series based on the triumphs and trials of Vinny Chase and his longtime friends.

368. This 1984 Cold War themed movie was the first movie to ever receive a PG-13 rating. Name it.

369. What is the fastest land animal on Earth?

370. Who was the youngest member of the Beatles?

371. During the election campaign season of 2008, which actress gained national attention for her impersonations of Sarah Palin?

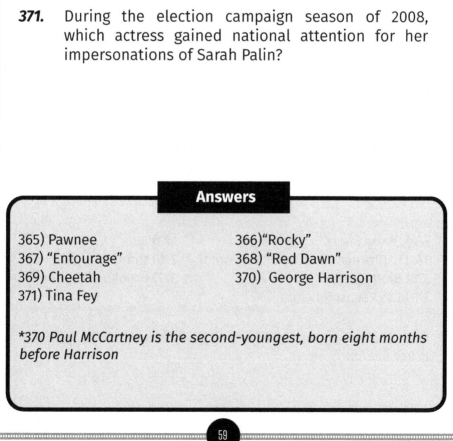

Answers

365) Pawnee
367) "Entourage"
369) Cheetah
371) Tina Fey

366)"Rocky"
368) "Red Dawn"
370) George Harrison

370 Paul McCartney is the second-youngest, born eight months before Harrison

372. In 2019, this song about a young creature of the sea became one of the few children's songs to ever appear in billboards top 100. Name it.

373. What was the first name of the character played by Michael J. Fox on the sitcom 'Family Ties?"

374. On the show "The Big Bang Theory," Leonard and Sheldon are both physicists at what university?

375. What is the third largest planet in the solar system?

376. If you are reading a book that begins with 921 in the Dewey Decimal System, what kind of book are you reading?

377. Name the duo with the first name Kix and Ronnie who were voted the top duo in country music every year between 1991 and 2006.

378. In what city was Tupac Shakur shot and killed?

Answers

372) "Baby Shark" 373) Alex
374) California Institute of Technology 375) Uranus
376) Biography 377) Brooks and Dunn
378) Las Vegas, Nevada

378- Shakur was murdered after a fight featuring Mike Tyson vs. Bruce Seldon

379. When Bob Marley sang "I Shot the Sheriff," who did he say he did not shoot?

380. Name the 1986 movie in which Steve Martin, Martin Short, and Chevy Chase played the title characters.

381. What is the most populated city in the United States to begin with the letter "D?"

382. Name the 2004 movie starring Clint Eastwood and Hilary Swank about a trainer trying to turn a woman into a successful boxer.

383. Which state is nicknamed "The Show Me State?"

384. Name the actor that played deputy Barney Fife on "The Andy Griffith" show.

385. What is the nickname for the athletic teams at Pepperdine University?

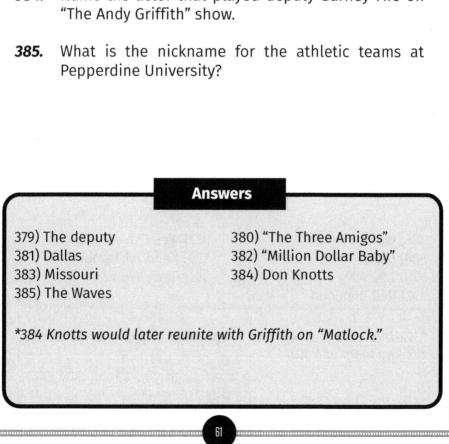

Answers

379) The deputy
381) Dallas
383) Missouri
385) The Waves

380) "The Three Amigos"
382) "Million Dollar Baby"
384) Don Knotts

*384 Knotts would later reunite with Griffith on "Matlock."

386. Name the singer whose hits included "Werewolves of London," "Poor Poor Pitiful Me," and "Lawyers, Guns, and Money."

387. Name the director of the movies "Nightmare on Elm Street," "The Hills Have Eyes," and "Scream."

388. During a division one football game, how many officials are on the field on each play?

389. Considered by many be one of the top rappers of 2020, he has won thirteen Grammies and is the only non-classical musician to be awarded the Pulitzer Prize for music. Name him.

390. In her hit single "Friday," what time does Rebecca Black wake up?

391. Which President is credited with coining the phrase, "the buck stops here?"

392. Name the famous singer who was once in the same high school choir as Barbara Streisand and attended N.Y.U. on a fencing scholarship.

Answers

386) Warren Zevon   387) Wes Craven
388) Eight   389) Kendrick Lamar
390) 7:00 A.M.   391) Harry Truman
392) Neil Diamond

392-Diamond was part of a national championship winning fencing team at N.Y.U.

393. On the hit television show "The Office," Michael Scott talks several times about his idea for a movie. What is the title of the movie he wants to make?

394. Name the basketball player who played at the University of South Carolina and then went on to score more points than any other NBA player in the decade of the 1980s.

395. In the movie "Ferris Bueller's Day Off," what Major League Baseball stadium do Ferris and his friends attend?

396. The Cape of Good Hope is the southernmost point on which continent?

397. Name the actress who played Dorothy in the 1939 film "The Wizard of Oz."

398. Who is the only coach in basketball history to win both an N.C.A.A. championship and an NBA title?

399. Name the actress who won an Academy Award in 1979 for "Kramer vs. Kramer," and another in 1982 for "Sophie's Choice."

Answers

393) "Threat Level Midnight"   394) Alex English
395) Wrigley Field   396) Africa
397) Judy Garland   398) Larry Brown
399- Meryl Streep

398- Brown won a NCAA championship at the University of Kansas, and a NBA championship with the Detroit Pistons

400. Name the author who wrote both "1984" and "Animal Farm."

401. With 11, which city has hosted the most Super Bowls?

402. In the 2005 film "Walk the Line," who was the actress who portrayed June Carter Cash?

403. Which U.S. president was the first to nominate an African American to serve as a U.S. Supreme Court Justice?

404. In 1994, when skater Nancy Kerrigan was attacked while leaving a practice facility, what city was she in?

405. Name the series which debuted in 2010 on the AMC network about the survivors of a zombie apocalypse.

406. What is the real name of hip hop star "Childish Gambino?"

Answers

400- George Orwell
402- Reece Witherspoon
404. Detroit, Michigan
406. Donald Glover

401- Miami
403- Lyndon B. Johnson
405- "The Walking Dead"

403- Johnson nominated Thurgood Marshall in 1967

407. World War Two in Europe began on September 1, 1939, when Poland was invaded by what country?

408. What college football coach led Notre Dame to a national championship in 1989?

409. Name the band whose debut album "How to Save a Life," released in 2005, included the top ten hit "Over My Head."

410. In what city is the hit TV show "Dexter" based?

411. In 1971, the London Bridge was taken apart in England and moved to which American state?

412. In Roman numerals, which letter represents the number 100?

413. The majority of season two of "Downton Abbey" takes place during which war?

Answers

407- Germany
409- The Fray
411- Arizona
413- World War One

408- Lou Holtz
410- Miami, Florida
412- C

414. Name the year in which both Adolph Hitler and Franklin D. Roosevelt died.

415. Name the hit television show which featured four female characters named Dorothy, Rose, Blanch, and Sofia.

416. What is the only letter not used to represent an element on the periodic table?

417. When James Bond orders martinis, he gives three words of instruction. What is the first of those three words?

418. Name the actor and comedian who serves as the unseen narrator on the TV show "How I Met Your Mother"?

419. From what city did the Fresh Prince move to Bel Air?

420. Which two states voted to become the first to legalize marijuana in the election of 2012?

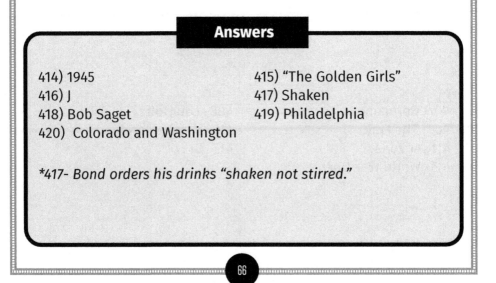

Answers

414) 1945
416) J
418) Bob Saget
420) Colorado and Washington

415) "The Golden Girls"
417) Shaken
419) Philadelphia

417- Bond orders his drinks "shaken not stirred."

421. Name the 2009 film which tells the story of Michael Oher, an offensive lineman for the Baltimore Ravens.

422. Between the years 2000 and 2010, the most-watched episode of any television show was the series finale of what sitcom?

423. Name the band who released albums in the 1990s with titles that included "Under the Table and Dreaming," "Crash," and "Before These Crowded Streets."

424. Name the ship that still rests at the bottom of Pearl Harbor and serves as a memorial accessed only by boat.

425. With what NBA team did Jerry Tarkanian once serve as the head coach?

426. Name the hip hop group that asked the question "Are you down with O.P.P.?" in 1992.

427. For which team did Bo Jackson take his final major league at bat in 1994?

Answers

421) "The Blind Side"
423) The Dave Matthews Band
425) San Antonio Spurs
427) California Angels

422) "Friends"
424) U.S.S. Arizona
426) Naughty By Nature

422- The finale of "Friends" aired May 6, 2004 and was watched by over 52 million viewers.

428. Name the 2001 movie today about a once abandoned janitor working at a Los Angeles radio station and trying to find his real family.

429. How many stomachs does a cow have?

430. Only two boxers who were heavyweight champions of the world shared the last name. What was it?

431. What is the name of the third installment of the "Fifty Shades" trilogy?

432. Of all players in the history of Major League Baseball, the NFL, and the NBA, who is the oldest person ever to win an M.V.P. award?

433. What was the last name of the U.S. president played by Martin Sheen in the series, "The West Wing?"

434. Whose album "Igor" won best rap album at the 62nd Grammy Awards in 2019?

Answers

428) "Joe Dirt"
430) Spinks
432) Tom Brady
434) Tyler, the Creator

429) Four
431) "Fifty Shades Freed"
433) Bartlett

* In 2018, at the age of 40 years and 6 months, Brady surpassed Barry Bonds by three months.

435. Name the author whose works include "In Cold Blood" and "Breakfast at Tiffany's."

436. Name the doctor played by Harrison Ford in the "Raiders of the Lost Ark" movie series.

437. In what city was the television show "Frasier" set?"

438. Name the band whose hits include "Rosanna,", "Africa," and "Hold the Line."

439. Name the actress that starred as Buffy in the "Buffy the Vampire Slayer" series from 1997 to 2003.

440. Who, at the age of 16, became the youngest female tennis player to ever win a grand slam event in 1994?

441. In 1924, what city became the first in the United States to have its own National Hockey League team?

Answers

435) Truman Capote
437) Seattle
439) Sarah Michelle Gellar
441) Boston, Massachusetts

436) Indiana Jones
438) Toto
440) Martina Hingis

442. Name the band comprised of Jack Black and Kyle Glass that released an album in 2006 titled "The Pick of Destiny?"

443. Name the actor who famously lip synced in his underwear in a movie to Bob Seger's "Old Time Rock and Roll."

444. Name the animated character whose famous catchphrase is "to infinity and beyond!"

445. Name the movie in which Jack Nicholson famously pronounces "Heeeeere's Johnny."

446. Who produced and performed in the 1989 "Batman" soundtrack that included the hits "Batdance" and "Partyman?"

447. Who was the first woman of color to win the Academy Award for best actress?

448. Name the first Disney movie to be adapted as a Broadway play, which happened in 1979.

Answers

442) Tenacious D
444) Buzz Lightyear
446) Prince
448) "Snow White"

443) Tom Cruise
445) "The Shining"
447) Halle Berry

447- Berry was awarded the 2002 Oscar for her role in "Monster's Ball."

449. Name the actor who starred in the movies "Bruce Almighty," "The Cable Guy," and "Me Myself and Irene."

450. Until 1988, Steve Perry served as the lead singer for which rock band?

451. Name the first president of the United States not to have the letter "A" in his last name.

452. Lake Victoria is the largest freshwater lake on which continent?

453. Name the rapper who was shot and killed on March 9, 1997, while in Los Angeles filming the video for his single "Hypnotize."

454. Name the actor who appeared in the movies "Superbad," "Knocked Up," "Forty-Year-Old Virgin" and who also once appeared on the cover of Playboy Magazine.

455. On the popular television show "N.C.I.S.," what does the "N' stand for?

Answers

449- Jim Carrey
451- Thomas Jefferson
453- Notorious B.I.G.
456- Naval

450- Journey
452- Africa
454- Seth Rogen

*455- "N.C.I.S." stands for "Naval Criminal Investigative Service"

457. Name the actress who made her debut on WB's "Seventh Heaven" in 1996 and would go on to star in movies such as "I Now Pronounce You Chuck and Larry" and "Summer Catch?"

458. She was born as Norma Jean Baker in 1926. By what name is she better known?

459. In the Harry Potter series, what are non-magicians known as?

460. Who had a No. 1 hit song in 2018 with "God's Plan?"

461. Ray Kinsella builds a baseball field on his farm in the movie "Field of Dreams." Which state was his farm in?

462. On the original Monopoly board, what is the most expensive piece of real estate?

463. Name the 2013 movie directed by Martin Scorsese which, as of 2020, held the Guinness record for most F-bombs in a single movie.

Answers

457) Jessica Biel   458) Marilyn Monroe
459) Muggles   460) Drake
461) Iowa   462) Boardwalk
463) "The Wolf of Wall Street"

* *The Wolf of Wall Street" has 569 "F bombs," and the 1999 film "Summer of Sam" is in second place with 435.*

464. Which is the least populated U.S. state?

465. Who was the first left handed NFL quarterback to be inducted into the Hall of Fame?

466. Where did former Dallas Cowboys quarterback Tony Romo play his college football?

467. Name the television show from which the phrase "jump the shark" originated.

468. What brand of toilet paper did Mr. Whipple ask viewers not to squeeze in television commercials that aired from 1964 to 1985?

469. Name the famous animated character who made his debut in the 1940 film "A Wild Hare."

470. According to the Gospel of Mark, what is the name of the Angel that tells the Virgin Mary she is pregnant?

Answers

464- Wyoming
466- Eastern Illinois
468- Charmin
470- Gabriel

465- Steve Young
467- "Happy Days"
469- Bugs Bunny

465- Steve Young was inducted into the hall of fame in 2005. Kenny Stabler is the only other left handed quarterback in the hall. Stabler was inducted in 2016.

471. How many squares are there on a chess board?

472. Name the actor who played Dr. John Becker on the TV series "Becker."

473. Name the NBA franchise which until 1999 played its home games in Market Square Arena.

474. Name the actress who burst onto the scene in 1980 with "Blue Lagoon" and was married to Tennis star Andre Agassi from 1997 to 1999.

475. Walter Mondale served as the vice president under which American president?

476. Name the actor who starred as Barney Stinson on "How I Met Your Mother" after playing the young doctor, Doogie Howser, from 1989 to 1993.

477. Name the Cleveland Indians slugger who had 165 runs batted in in 1999, the most by any major leaguer in 60 years?

Answers

471) 64

473) Indiana Pacers

475) Jimmy Carter

477) Manny Ramirez

472) Ted Danson

474) Brooke Shields

476) Neal Patrick Harris

478. Name the artist who released her seventh No. 1 album in 2020 titled "Folklore."

479. What is the chemical symbol for iron?

480. In 1986, which journalist hosted a two-hour prime time special titled "The Mystery of Al Capone's Vault?"

481. As of 2020, which hip hop star has won more Grammies than any other male artist in the 21st century?

482. In the song "American Pie" by Don Mclean, when "the jester sang for the king and queen," whose coat was he wearing?

483. Name the comedian/actor who has appeared in the movies "Ride Along," "Central Intelligence,", "The Wedding Ringer," and "Get Hard."

484. Name the actor whose television hits include "Arrested Development," "Ozark," and "Valerie."

Answers

478) Taylor Swift
480) Geraldo Rivera
482) James Dean
484) Jason Bateman

479) Fe
481) Kanye West
483) Kevin Hart

481- West has won 14, Beyonce and Allison Krause are tied for the most overall with 16.

485. Who has appeared in more NBA games than any other player?

486. Name the country music artist whose 1990 album "No Fences" included the hits "Friends In Low Places," "The Thunder Rolls," and "Unanswered Prayers."

487. Name the Seattle Mariner who in 2001 was named the Rookie of the Year and the American League Most Valuable Player.

488. How many years were there between the end of George H.W. Bush's presidency and the start of George W. Bush's presidency?

489. Name the 1997 movie in which six unemployed steel workers form a male striptease act.

490. On the campus of which Ivy league school was the social media platform "Facebook" created.

491. Name the Rapper who was born as Cornell Iral Haynes Jr.. His albums include, "Sweat", "Brass knuckles" and "Suit".

Answers

485) Robert Parish
487) Ichiro Suzuki
489) "The Full Monty"
491) Nelly

486) Garth Brooks
488) Eight
490) Harvard

485- Parish appeared in 1611 games. Kareem Abdul Jabbar is second with 1560.

492. Steve Prefontaine was a long distance running star at which University in the early 1970's?

493. What does the Q stand for in the magazine *GQ*?

494. How many sides does a rhombus have?

495. Who was the first Republican president of the United States?

496. Name the pop music icon who died the day before the 2012 Grammies.

497. Both with 7, which two NFL franchises have had the very first pick in the NFL draft the most times?

498. Name the country music singer whose album "Blue" went No. 1 in 1996 while she was only 13 years old.

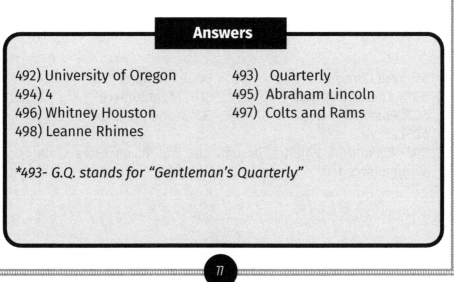

Answers

492) University of Oregon
494) 4
496) Whitney Houston
498) Leanne Rhimes

493) Quarterly
495) Abraham Lincoln
497) Colts and Rams

493- G.Q. stands for "Gentleman's Quarterly"

499. Who was the first American president to visit Vietnam after the Vietnam War?

500. In "Beauty and the Beast," what is the name of Belle's horse?

501. Name the 1964 children's book written by Shel Silverstein about the relationship between a boy and an apple tree.

502. Name the city in Alabama that was once the capital of the confederacy.

503. Name the popular 21st century musician who has the words "always tired" tattooed below his eyes.

504. Name the author whose works include "The Grapes of Wrath," "Travels With Charley," and "Of Mice and Men."

505. In College football games which feature overtime, on what yard line do the teams begin their overtime possession?

Answers

499) Bill Clinton
501) "The Giving Tree"
503) Post Malone
505) 25

500) Phillippe
502) Montgomery
504) John Steinbeck

502- *Richmond, Virginia, became the capital once the state of Virginia seceded.*

506. In which war did the most Americans lose their lives?

507. What school did Jim Valvano lead to a college basketball national championship in 1983?

508. Name the quarterback taken second in the 1998 draft by the San Diego Chargers and is often considered to be the worst high draft pick in NFL history.

509. Name the character played by Robert Wagner in all three Austin Powers films.

510. Name the musical created by the creators of "South Park" which made its Broadway debut in 2011.

511. In 1992, this became the first state to elect two women to the U.S. Senate.

512. In 2015, Taylor Swift became only the second woman to win Billboard's artist of the year award for a second time. Who was the first?

Answers

506) The Civil War
508) Ryan Leaf
510) "The Book of Mormon"
512) Adele

507) North Carolina State
509) Number Two
511) California

511- In 1993, Diane Feinstein and Barbara Boxer began representing the state of California in the Senate together.

513. Who famously wore a T-shirt saying "corporate magazines still suck" on the cover of Rolling Stone magazine?

514. Name the singer whose hits include "Pretty Woman,","Only the Lonely," and "Anything You Want."

515. Name the female singer who jumped from the top of Houston's N.R.G. stadium at halftime of the 2017 Superbowl.

516. Name the 1897 novel by Bram Stoker which has since been referenced in over 600 movie titles worldwide.

517. Name the town in South Dakota in which Calamity Jane and Wild Bill Hickock are buried.

518. Name the hit single by the band Bow Wow Wow which placed at No. 86 on VH1's list of the 100 greatest songs of the 1980s.

519. Name the band whose debut album in 2004 was titled "Hot Fuss" and included the hits "Smile Like You Mean It," "Mr. Brightside," and "Jenny Was a Friend of Mine."

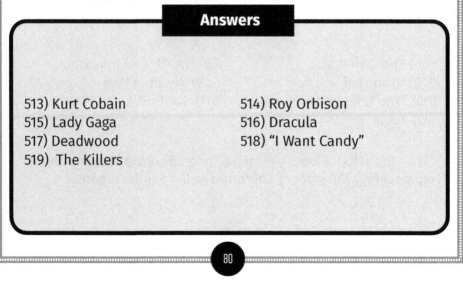

Answers

513) Kurt Cobain
515) Lady Gaga
517) Deadwood
519) The Killers

514) Roy Orbison
516) Dracula
518) "I Want Candy"

520. Name the actor who played boxer Butch Coolidge in the 1994 film "Pulp Fiction."

521. Name the band whose album titled "The Wall" was the best-selling album of the 1970's.

522. The state of New York is known as the _____ state.

523. What was the last name of the judge that presided over the People of California vs. O.J. Simpson trial in 1995?

524. What is the most populous city in New Hampshire?

525. When people suffer from sleep apnea, they are often directed to use a C.P.A.P. machine. What does the final "P" in "C.P.A.P." stand for?

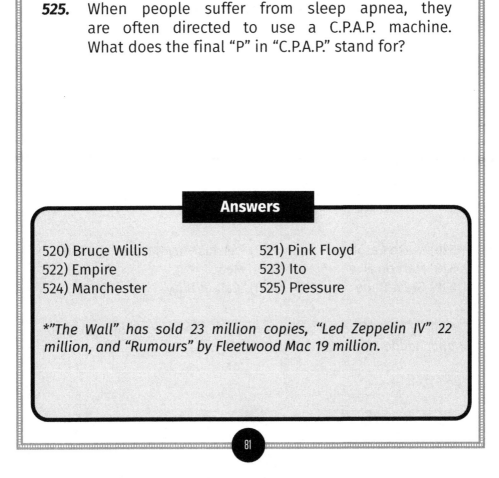

Answers

520) Bruce Willis   521) Pink Floyd
522) Empire   523) Ito
524) Manchester   525) Pressure

"The Wall" has sold 23 million copies, "Led Zeppelin IV" 22 million, and "Rumours" by Fleetwood Mac 19 million.

526. Name the state which has license plates proclaiming "First in Flight."

527. Name the boxer who was stripped of his heavyweight title because he refused to fight in the Vietnam war.

528. Name the colorful band whose hits include "Harder to Breathe," "She Will Be Loved," and "Moves Like Jagger."

529. When chili is served "con carne," what does it include?

530. What breed of dog is Scooby Doo?

531. What was the highest selling video game of 2019?

Answers

526) North Carolina   527) Cassius Clay (Muhammad Ali)
528) Maroon Five   529) Meat
530) Great Dane   531) "Call of Duty"

Call of Duty: Modern Warfare was followed closely by NBA 2k20 and Madden N.F.L. 20

532. Name the comedy duo whose 1978 film "Up in Smoke" would become a cult classic.

533. Name the fellow star that joined Madonna in a controversial kiss during the 2003 M.T.V. video music awards.

534. Which band was featured making a new record in the famous "Saturday Night Live" skit, "More Cowbell?"

535. In 2009, who became the first Hispanic-American to serve on the United States Supreme Court?

536. In what city is the hit television series "Seinfeld" based?

537. Name the 1967 movie with the famous quote, "What we've got here is failure to communicate."

538. Name the golfer nicknamed "The Walrus," who won the 1982 Masters.

Answers

532) Cheech and Chong

533) Britney Spears

534) Blue Oyster Cult

535) Sonia Sotomayor

536) New York City

537) "Cool Hand Luke"

538) Craig Stadler

535- Sotomayor was nominated by Barack Obama in 2009.

539. Chelsey "Sully" Sullenberger gained international fame in 2009 for evacuating passengers after his plane crashed into a river. What river did the plane crash into?

540. Who was the host of "American Top 40" from 1970 to 2014?

541. Name the famous Mexican-American singer who was murdered by the founder of her fan club in 1995.

542. Name the hit TV show that aired from 1989 to 1993 and featured Zach, A.C., Kelly, and Screech, all students of Bayside High.

543. Name the former U.S. Secretary of State and Democratic presidential nominee who served as a U.S. Senator from New York from 2001 to 2009.

544. The daughter of what famous singer was married to Michael Jackson from 1994 to 1996?

545. The television show "Orange is the New Black" is based on life in a fictional prison. What state is that prison in?

Answers

539) The Hudson   540) Casey Kasem
541) Selena   542) "Saved By the Bell"
543) Hillary Clinton   544) Elvis Presley
545) New York

546. Name the NFL team which plays its home games at the highest altitude.

547. Name the restaurant chain who uses the slogan "Eatin' Good in the Neighborhood."

548. What was the first name of the oldest daughter in the Anderson family on the classic sit-com "Father Knows Best?"

549. What is the name of the candle display used by Jewish people during Hanukkah?

550. Who was the girl whose phone number was 867-5309 in the song by Tommy Tutone?

551. Name the TV show that aired from 1984 to 1989 starring Don Johnson and Phillip Michael Thomas as South Florida detectives.

552. What did Disneyland begin selling to the general public inside the park for the first time in 2019?

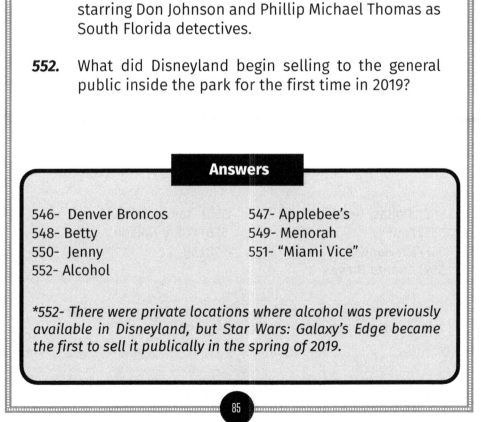

Answers

546- Denver Broncos   547- Applebee's
548- Betty   549- Menorah
550- Jenny   551- "Miami Vice"
552- Alcohol

552- There were private locations where alcohol was previously available in Disneyland, but Star Wars: Galaxy's Edge became the first to sell it publically in the spring of 2019.

553. In what city was President John F. Kennedy assassinated?

554. Cinco de Mayo celebrates an important Mexican military victory on May 5, 1862. Which country did the Mexican army defeat that day?

555. To be known as a colt, a horse must be under _____ years of age.

556. Name the country music legend who celebrates two birthdays: April 29 and April 30.

557. What was the name of the history teacher played by Ray Walton in the film "Fast Times at Ridgemont High?"

558. In the game of Yahtzee, how many points do you get if you roll your first Yahtzee of the game?

559. Starting in 1991, which National League baseball team won 14 straight division titles?

Answers

553) Dallas, Texas   554) France
555) Four   556) Willie Nelson
557) Mr. Hand   558) 50
559) Atlanta Braves

554- Many people confuse Cinco de Mayo with Mexican Independence Day, which is September 16.

560. In F.I.F.A., the World Cup soccer governing organization, what does the first '"F" stand for?

561. According to the Cure's 1992 hit single, on what day of the week did the singer fall in love?

562. In the movie "Pocahontas," what is the name of the pug who has his own carousel with dog biscuits?

563. Name the gymnast who won five gold medals while representing Romania as a 14-year-old at the 1976 Olympics.

564. Name the show based on culinary competitions that premiered on the Bravo network in 2006.

565. May 4th is considered a day of celebration for fans of which movie series?

566. Chris Martin is the lead singer for which highly successful 21st century band?

Answers

560) Federation
562) Percy
564) "Top Chef"
566) Coldplay

561) Friday
563) Nadia Comici
565) Star Wars

560- "F.I.F.A." stands for "Federation Internationale de Football Association"

567. If a golfer shoots what is nicknamed a "snowman" on a hole, how many shots did it take to complete the hole?

568. Which American city is often referred to at "Motown?"

569. Name the popular 1990s band whose hits include "Semi-Charmed Life," "Jumper," and "How's it Gonna Be?"

570. In "Angry Birds," what color are the pigs from which the birds are trying to save their eggs?

571. On May 4, 1970, at which university were four protesters shot at killed by the U.S. National Guard?

572. Which country music singer had the hit single "Stays in Mexico," which went to No. 3 on the country music charts in 2004?

573. Hogback Mountain is the highest peak in which state?

Answers

567) Eight
569) Third Eye Blind
571) Kent State
573) Nebraska

568) Detroit
570) Green
572) Toby Keith

568- Because of its status as a world leader in the automobile industry, Detroit is often referred to as the "Motor City."

574. Which Major League baseball team plays its home games at Tropicana Field?

575. Name the only state to share a border with only one other state?

576. "We love to fly and it shows" is whose airline slogan?

577. Which is the only Disney animated film in which the title character does not speak?

578. What sitcom aired on ABC from 1986 to 1993 and was based on a rocky relationship between two cousins named Larry and Balky?

579. Who was known as the "Godfather of Soul," with hits including "Living in America" and "I Feel Good?"

580. Before embarking on her successful solo career, what band did Gwen Stefani once lead?

Answers

574) Tampa Bay Rays

575) Maine

576) Delta

577) "Dumbo"

578) "Perfect Strangers"

579) James Brown

580) No Doubt

581. With eight, which state has produced the most United States presidents?

582. What was the name of the supergroup which included Roy Orbison, Tom Petty, George Harrison, Jeff Lynne, and Bob Dylan?

583. In which city was Martin Luther King, Jr., murdered?

584. What is the name of the 2016 movie in which Wade Wilson hunts down a man who gave him a scarred appearance?

585. Before moving to Soldier Field in 1970, in what stadium did the Chicago Bears play their home games?

586. Which is the only of the Great Lakes to be located entirely within the United States?

587. As of 2020, what is the highest grossing film of all time?

Answers

581) Virginia
583) Memphis
585) Wrigley Field
587) "Avatar"

582) The Traveling Wilburys
584) "Deadpool"
586) Lake Michigan

*581- George Washington, Thomas Jefferson, James Madison, James Monroe, William Henry Harrison, John Tyler, Zachary Taylor and Woodrow Wilson.

588. Name the only state that begins with the letter "A" but does not end with it.

589. Name the actor who played the character of Alan Harper on "Two and a Half Men."

590. What does the "B" in BMW stand for?

591. Who, in 1982, became the youngest person to ever host "Saturday Night Live," at age 7?

592. Of all the countries in the "G20," or group of 20, which one comes first alphabetically?

593. What was the last name of the captain of "The Love Boat?"

594. Name the 2008 film about two grown men who are forced to live together after their parents marry.

Answers

588) Arkansas

589) Jon Cryer

590) Bavarian (*Bayerische*)

591) Drew Barrymore

592) Argentina

593) Stubing

594) Stepbrothers

591- Macaulay Culkin is the second youngest, hosting at the age of 11.

595. What is the last name shared by a fictional overaged elementary student and a real founding father who later became an American president.

596. Name the NFL team which won four of the first 14 Super Bowls.

597. Which singer was the most-streamed artist on Spotify in 2019?

598. What is the name of Bob Seger's backup band?

599. Which famous actor had his breakout performance as a young, developmentally disabled man in 1993's "What's Eating Gilbert Grape?"

600. What was the name of the first permanent English settlement in North America?

601. In 1985, who became the first man to ever be named "Sexiest Man Alive"?

Answers

595) Madison
597) Post Malone
599) Leonardo DiCaprio
601) Mel Gibson

596) Pittsburgh Steelers
598) The Silver Bullet Band
600) Jamestown

*597- 1. Post Malone, 2. Billie Eilish, 3. Ariana Grande, 4. Ed Sheeran, 5. Bad Bunny

602. In what state did Elvis Presley die?

603. Of the seven continents, which has the fewest square miles?

604. Which state is the only one that you can type while using the letters from only one row on the keyboard?

605. What was the fictional coffee shop featured on the television show "Friends?"

606. Name the comedian who became famous because of his "Seven Words You Can Never Say On Television" routine.

607. Name the American rock band who had hits in 2009 with "Sex on Fire" and "Use Somebody."

608. Name the game show that aired on the Discovery channel beginning in 2005, hosted by stand up comedian Ben Bailey.

Answers

602) Tennessee
604) Alaska
606) George Carlin
608) "Cash Cab"

603) Australia
605) Central Perk
607) Kings of Leon

609. Name the film from the year 2000 about two rival cheerleading teams named the Clovers and the Toros.

610. What is the normal number of teeth for an adult human to have?

611. Whose song titled "The Shape of You" is the most-streamed song in the history of Spotify, as of 2020?

612. Who has won the most titles as an NBA head coach?

613. Thom Delong formed the group Angels and Airwaves after the band in which he was lead singer broke up in 2005. Name that band.

614. Which famous American monument did 21-year-old Yale University student Maya Lin design in 1981?

615. Who is the only player in Major League Baseball history to hit 500 home runs and steal 500 bases?

Answers

609) "Bring it On"
611) Ed Sheeran
613) Blink 182
615) Barry Bonds

610) 32
612) Phil Jackson
614) Vietnam Wall

612- Phil Jackson has won 11. Red Auerbach is second with 9.

616. Which American president signed the legislation that created Medicare?

617. Name the singer who reached No. 2 on the billboard top 100 in 1996 with the song "I Believe I Can Fly," from the soundtrack to the movie "Space Jam."

618. For which movie did Steven Spielberg win his first Academy Award for best director?

619. What model of car did David Hasselhoff drive in his hit show "Knight Rider?"

620. Name the college football program that appeared in every season ending AP Top 25 poll from 1969 to 2001.

621. What was Nancy Reagan's three-word slogan used in the fight against drug use in the 1980's?

622. Name the band that had a No. 1 hit on the "Rocky Three" soundtrack with "Eye of the Tiger."

Answers

616) Lyndon Johnson
618) "Schindler's List"
620) University of Nebraska
622) Survivor

617) R. Kelly
619) Trans Am
621) Just Say No

620- The University of Michigan has the second longest streak, with 20. (1985-2004)

623. Name the 1955 animated movie which famously featured two dogs romantically sharing a plate of spaghetti and meatballs.

624. What was the name of the punk band that featured members named DeeDee, Joey, Johnny, and Tommy?

625. Which network began using the peacock as its symbol in 1956?

626. In addition to owning the Seattle Supersonics, what major American beverage company did Howard Schultz once serve as the CEO?

627. Only one NFL player has ever been named the MVP five times. Name him.

628. In terms of the televised shopping network, what does "Q.V.C." stand for?

629. Which major religion features the "Five Pillars of Faith?"

Answers

623) "The Lady and the Tramp" 624) The Ramones
625) N.B.C. 626) Starbucks
627) Peyton Manning 628) Quality, Value, Convenience
629) Islam

630. What is the most populated city in the state of Delaware?

631. A "fifth of whiskey" is one-fifth of which: a gallon, quart, or liter?

632. What sport uses epees, foils, and sabers?

633. Who was automatically your first friend when you joined Myspace?

634. Of the four teams in the NFL's AFC South division, which one is located furthest north?

635. "The Jeffersons" was a spin-off of what popular American television show?

636. In the year 2000, for which team did Dennis Rodman play his final NBA game?

Answers

630) Wilmington
632) Fencing
634) Indianapolis Colts
636) Dallas Mavericks

631) A gallon
633) Tom
635) "All In the Family"

635- "All in the Family" had seven spinoffs, the most of any television show.

637. In what country would you find the state of Punjab?

638. What does G.M.O. stand for?

639. Name the popular app in which users can send pictures to each other which debuted July 8, 2011.

640. Which Heavy Metal band has sold more albums than any other?

641. Which state averages the most tornados?

642. In 1961, Jean Neditch began inviting friends over to discuss health and fitness once a week. Those meetings would lead to the founding of _____ , which now has more than one million members.

643. Moraine Lake is in which Canadian province?

Answers

637) India
639) Snapchat
641) Texas
643) Alberta

638) Genetically Modified Organisms
640) Metallica
642) Weight Watchers

641- Kansas is second, followed by Florida and Oklahoma.

644. By what name is convicted criminal Theodore Kaczynski better known?

645. Name the program that debuted on M.T.V. in 1992 about a group of strangers living in a loft, which is considered the first modern "reality" show on television.

646. On the periodic table, what is the symbol for gold?

647. Between the years 2000 and 2020, which college football program had the most players taken in the first round of the NFL draft?

648. Name the show about a man being able to choose from a pool of potential romantic interests that began airing on ABC in 2002.

649. Name the artist whose 1992 live album became the greatest selling live album of all time.

650. Name the deceased musician who magically re-appeared as a hologram at Coachella in 2012?

Answers

644) The Unabomber
646) AU
648) "The Bachelor"
650) Tupac Shakur

645) "The Real World"
647) Florida State University
649) Eric Clapton

644- "Unabomber" comes from the F.B.I. referring to the suspect as the "University and Airline Bomber."

651. In the 1980 Winter Olympics, which country did the United States hockey team defeat in the gold medal final?

652. The "won" is the official currency of which country?

653. Who is the oldest of the Kardashian sisters?

654. Which state is known as "The Garden State?"

655. Over half of the world's olive oil is produced in which country?

656. In what American city would you find "The Gateway Arch?"

657. Who was the Democratic nominee for president in 2004?

Answers

651) Finland
653) Kourtney
655) Spain
657) John Kerry

652) South Korea
654) New Jersey
656) St. Louis

651- The famous "Miracle On Ice" win over the Soviet Union was the semi-final game.

658. Which country has the most miles of coastline?

659. Which is the southernmost team in the National Hockey League?

660. Which female singer released a popular duet with Tom Petty in 1981 titled "Stop Draggin' My Heart Around?"

661. Name the actor who once played the role of Superman and who was paralyzed in an accident during a 1995 equestrian competition.

662. "Parrotheads" are the loyal fan base of which singer?

663. Sofia is the capital of which European country?

664. What was the title of Michelle Obama's 2018 best-selling autobiography?

Answers

658) Canada

659) Florida Panthers

660) Stevie Nicks

661) Christopher Reeve

662) Jimmy Buffet

663) Bulgaria

664) "Becoming"

665. Name the only state which does not have an athletic team that competes at the college division one level?

666. Give the title to the classic hit by the rock band Van Halen that begins with the line "I live my life like there's no tomorrow."

667. What does the "C" in C.A.T. scan stand for?

668. Which former heavyweight boxing champion was nicknamed "The Real Deal?"

669. Name the country music group that had a hit in 2006 with a cover of the song "Life Is a Highway" released on the soundtrack to the movie "Cars."

670. In the 1992 movie "Wayne's World," whose rock concert do Wayne and Garth attend?

671. Name the author that created the James Bond series.

Answers

665) Alaska

666) "Running With the Devil"

667) Computerized

668) Evander Holyfield

669) Rascal Flats

670) Alice Cooper

671) Ian Fleming

"C.A.T." stands for Computerized Axial Tomography

672. What word entered the Oxford English Dictionary in 2014 and is thought to have been invented by an Australian man after a drunken night out.

673. One of two original founders of a major department store chain died when the Titanic sank in 1912. Name the department store.

674. This iconic American structure opened in California in 1937 and cost 50 cents to travel. Name it.

675. In which state would you find North Cascades National Park?

676. Which is the only American state to have only one syllable in its name?

677. Under which president was the Department of Homeland Security created?

678. Name the actress who played Denise Huxtable on "The Cosby Show" and later married rock Musician Lenny Kravitz.

Answers

672) Selfie

673) Macy's

674) Golden Gate Bridge

675) Washington

676) Maine

677) George W. Bush

678) Lisa Bonet

679. Name the 2018 film starring Bradley Cooper and Lady Gaga which was nominated for eight Academy Awards.

680. If a person goes into a cardiac or respiratory arrest at a medical facility, medical staff will refer to this as a code _____.

681. Name the animated show on Nickelodeon about a dimwitted cat and an unstable chihuahua that aired from 1991 to 1995.

682. Name the city in Arizona with Standing on the Corner City Park.

683. In the cartoon strip "Peanuts," what is Charlie Brown's sister's name?

684. Name the disco singer that had a No. 1 hit in the late 1970's with "I Will Survive."

685. In the movie "Who Framed Roger Rabbit," who did the voice of the character of Jessica Rabbit?

Answers

679) "A Star is Born"
681) Ren and Stimpy
683) Sally
685) Kathleen Turner

680) Blue
682) Winslow
684) Gloria Gaynor

682- This is because of the line from the Eagles hit "Take it Easy:" "Now I'm a-standing on a corner in Winslow, Arizona, with such a fine sight to see."

686. Name the band for which Chrissie Hynde served as the lead singer and whose hits include "Brass in Pocket," "I'll Stand By You," and "Back on the Chain Gang."

687. In 2014, a group of hackers broke into Sony Pictures' computer network. They demanded that a movie not be released. Which movie?

688. In terms of square miles, what is the largest state east of the Mississippi river?

689. Name the Baseball Hall of Fame pitcher who was also drafted by the Los Angeles Kings in the 1984 NHL draft.

690. As of 2020, the most-liked picture in the history of Instagram has been of what object?

691. Whose song titled "Candy Shop" was the most popular ringtone of 2009?

692. Name the only actor to be nominated for an Emmy for playing the same character on three different television shows.

Answers

686) The Pretenders
688) Michigan
690) An egg
692) Kelsey Grammar

687) "The Interview"
689) Tom Glavine
691) 50 Cent

692- Grammar was nominated for his role as Frasier Crane in the shows Cheers, Frasier, and in a cameo appearance on the show "Wings."

693. Name the comedic pair who took an excellent adventure, had a bogus journey, and in 2020 returned to face the music.

694. Name the English singer who won the 2019 Grammy for best new artist.

695. Name the band whose second album, titled "Fashion Nugget" in 1996, included the song "The Distance," which dominated radio that fall.

696. On the popular sitcom "Family Matters," what was Steve's last name?

697. In which state would one find the Pro Football Hall of Fame?

698. Name the country music singer whose hits include "I Go Back," "No Shoes, No Shirt, No Problems," and "The Good Stuff."

699. Which state shares the longest border with Canada?

Answers

693) Bill and Ted

694) Dua Lipa

695) Cake

696) Urkel

697) Ohio

698) Kenny Chesney

699) Alaska

700. Name the former lead singer of Credence Clearwater Revival who had a solo hit with "Centerfield."

701. What is the more commonly known last name of the 2020 cultural sensation whose birth name is Joseph Allen Maldonado-Passage.

702. In what state was the famous final scene of the movie "Thelma and Louise" filmed?

703. Name the "Saturday Night Live" cast member who was shot and killed by his wife in 1998.

704. The twitter account for KFC allows only six men to follow the account. They all have the same first name. What is that first name?

705. In which state would you find the lowest elevation in the United States?

706. What series did Steve Irwin host on the Animal Planet from 1997 to 2004?

Answers

700) John Fogerty
702) Utah
704) Herb
706) "The Crocodile Hunter"

701) Exotic
703) Phil Hartman
705) California

704- KFC proudly boasts of 11 secret herbs and spices in their recipe.

707. When "Rolling Stone Magazine" published its list of the 100 greatest albums of the 1980s, "London Calling" was Number 1. Name the band which released it.

708. Which band is comprised of a brother and sister and in 2003 gave us the stadium anthem "Seven Nation Army."

709. In the television show, "The Addams Family," Morticia and Gomez have two children. One is named Pugsley. Who is the other?

710. What is the name of the actor who was the voice of both Mufasa in "The Lion King" and Darth Vader in "Star Wars?"

711. In the 1998 remake of the movie "The Parent Trap," which young actress played both characters Annie and Hailie?

712. Name the famous New York Yankee who in 1977 earned the nickname "Mr. October."

713. Name the college football program that has the honor of having both the youngest and oldest Heisman trophy winners ever.

Answers

707) The Clash

708) The White Stripes

709) Wednesday

710) James Earl Jones

711) Lindsay Lohan

712) Reggie Jackson

713) Florida State University

707- 1. London Calling, 2. "Purple Rain"- Prince, 3. "The Joshua Tree"- U2

714. Who was the only African-American man to win an Emmy, Grammy, Oscar, and Tony award?

715. When a hostage develops a bond with the captors, it is known as _____ syndrome.

716. Tommy, Chuckie, and Angelica were stars of which Nickelodeon cartoon?

717. In the "Rocky" movie series, what is Rocky's wife's first name?

718. In which state were the first shots of the American revolution fired?

719. Who was the host of the first 28 seasons of "Dancing With the Stars?"

720. In what state was Gatorade invented?

Answers

714) John Legend

715) Stockholm

716) "Rugrats"

717) Adrian

718) Massachusetts

719) Tom Bergeron

720) Florida

720- "Gatorade" was invented by researchers at the University of Florida (mascot: Gators) to help athletes replenish their electrolyte supply during and after games and practices.

721. Name the pop star who is godmother to both of Elton John's sons.

722. His friends in high school in Minnesota called him Sparky even though his first name was Charles. He went on to be one of the most successful cartoonists of all time. What is his last name?

723. In the song "I've Been Everywhere," what is the first city or town mentioned by Johnny Cash?

724. Ray Bradbury chose the title 451 Fahrenheit for the title of his famous novel because that is the temperature at which a _____ will begin to burn without being lit.

725. Name the 1980 movie starring Jane Fonda, Lily Tomlin, and Dolly Parton about three females working for a sexist, egotistical bigot played by Dabney Coleman.

726. What country were both Pakistan and Bangladesh once a part of?

727. Name the comedy duo which gave us the character of Mr. Garvey, an angry substitute teacher who struggles to correctly pronounce student's names.

Answers

721) Lady Gaga

722) Schulz

723) Winnemucca

724) Book

725) Nine to Five

726) Pakistan

727) Key and Peale

726- At the time, Bangladesh was known as "East Pakistan"

728. Name the 1980s band whose hits included "Down Under" and "Who Can it Be Now?"

729. In the movie "The Big Lebowski," for which legendary band did The Dude say he was once a roadie?

730. Who hosted a show on the Discovery Channel titled "Dirty Jobs" from 2003 to 2012?

731. In 1962-63, Terry Baker became the only man to ever win the Heisman Trophy for college football and also play in the Final Four in college basketball. Which university did he attend?

732. Ken Jennings famously had a 74-game winning streak on which television game show?

733. Name the publisher who is entombed in a vault next to Marilyn Monroe.

734. The rock band AC/DC's name is an acronym. What do both C's stand for?

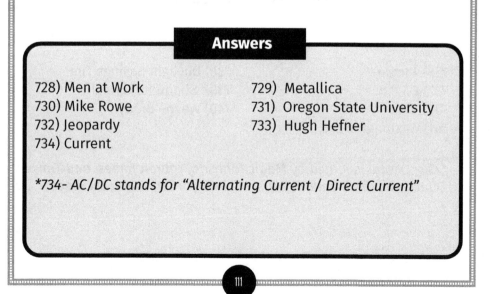

Answers

728) Men at Work

730) Mike Rowe

732) Jeopardy

734) Current

729) Metallica

731) Oregon State University

733) Hugh Hefner

*734- AC/DC stands for "Alternating Current / Direct Current"

735. Born in 1904, Johhny Weismuller won five Olympic gold medals in swimming, and also starred as what famous character in movies 12 times?

736. Although it was first suggested by Benjamin Franklin in the 1770s, what was not officially observed in America until 1918?

737. Name the cable television network that made its debut in 1979 by showing a professional softball game.

738. Name the player who was named MVP of the NBA finals in the 2000, 2001, and 2002 seasons.

739. Give the current name of the singer who was born as Alecia Beth Moore and in 2002 won MTVs best female video and best dance video with "Get This Party Started."

740. Name the actor/comedian who was a regular on "Whose Line Is It Anyway," and who has hosted "Let's Make a Deal" and "Don't Forget the Lyrics."

741. If you left Virginia and crossed the Francis Scott Key Bridge, in what city would you arrive?

Answers

735) Tarzan
737) E.S.P.N.
739) Pink
741) Washington D.C.

736) Daylight Savings Time
738) Shaquille O'Neal
740) Wayne Brady

738- O'Neal is joined by Magic Johnson, Lebron James, and Tim Duncan as three time winners. Michael Jordan won it six times.

742. Name the singer who gave birth to twins Rumi and Sir in June, 2017.

743. The Suez Canal connects the Mediterranean Sea to what body of water?

744. What was the name of the person who was found murdered alongside Nicole Brown Simpson in June, 1994?

745. Name the denomination of Christianity that was founded by John Wesley in 1738.

746. Eminem's song "Lose Yourself" was featured in which movie, starring Eminem?

747. Which singer won the very first "American Idol" competition in 2002?

748. What was the last name of Fred Flintstone's boss?

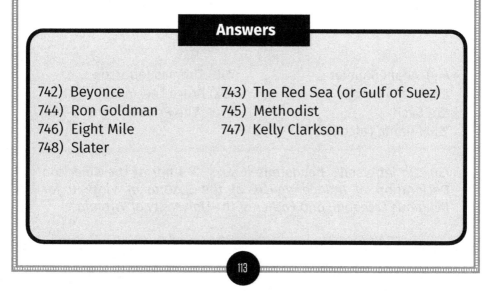

Answers

742) Beyonce

744) Ron Goldman

746) Eight Mile

748) Slater

743) The Red Sea (or Gulf of Suez)

745) Methodist

747) Kelly Clarkson

749. Which "Saturday Night Live" cast member made regular appearances at the "Weekend Update" desk as both "Opera Man" and "Cajun Man?"

750. On which former president's headstone does it say "Father of the University of Virginia?"

751. In the spring of 1983, the No. 1 song in America was "What a Feeling" by Irene Cara. What movie soundtrack did it appear first on?

752. Name the martial arts and film legend who died at the age of 32 and is now buried in Seattle, Washington, next to his son.

753. What is the name of the reindeer in the 2013 film, "Frozen?"

754. As of 2020, what is the longest running game show in television history?

755. Only one Super Bowl in history has gone into overtime. Name the losing team in that game.

Answers

749) Adam Sandler
751) "Flashdance"
753) Sven
755) Atlanta Falcons

750) Thomas Jefferson
752) Bruce Lee
754) "The Price is Right"

750- On Jefferson's headstone it says, "Author of the American Declaration of Independence, of the Statute of Virginia for Religious Freedom, and Father of the University of Virginia."

756. What city does the professional soccer team named "The Earthquakes" call home?

757. Name the northern European country that in 1907 became the very first in the world to give women the right to vote.

758. Three major rock stars, each aged 27, died within ten months of each other in 1970-71. Jim Morrison, Jimi Hendrix, and who?

759. Name the fictional town in which the "Andy Griffith Show" was set.

760. In what year did Mt. St. Helens erupt, causing the deaths of 57 people?

761. Name the TV show which debuted in 2009 on the Fox network about trying to bring a school extracurricular program back to its former glory?

762. Superstar Cherilyn Sarkisian was born in 1946. By what one word is she better known as?

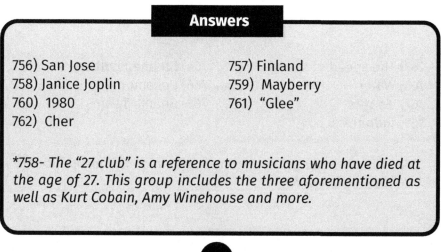

Answers

756) San Jose   757) Finland
758) Janice Joplin   759) Mayberry
760) 1980   761) "Glee"
762) Cher

*758- The "27 club" is a reference to musicians who have died at the age of 27. This group includes the three aforementioned as well as Kurt Cobain, Amy Winehouse and more.

763. If something is flying at "Mach 10," this means it is flying at a rate of ten multiplied by what?

764. Name the comedian who left Comedy Central's "Daily Show" to begin hosting his own nightly show in 2005?

765. In "The Wizard of Oz," what causes the Wicked Witch of the West to melt?

766. Name the app which was a monster hit in 2016 and has been credited with teaching millions of Americans the metric system.

767. Built for the 1962 World's Fair, which American city is host to the world's oldest operating revolving restaurant?

768. Which female singer has the highest selling country music studio album of all time with "Come on Over."

769. Name the highest populated country located entirely within the southern hemisphere.

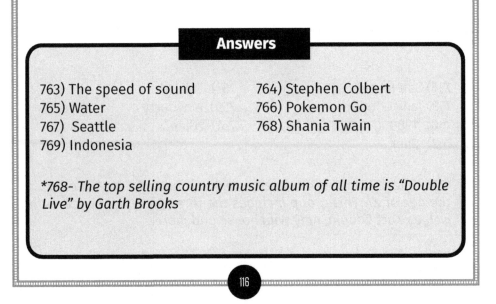

Answers

763) The speed of sound
765) Water
767) Seattle
769) Indonesia

764) Stephen Colbert
766) Pokemon Go
768) Shania Twain

768- The top selling country music album of all time is "Double Live" by Garth Brooks

770. What is the name of the country music singer who starred in the movie "Pure Country?"

771. Name the Super Bowl winning quarterback who makes a cameo appearance in the 1998 film, "There's Something About Mary."

772. Name the former football and baseball player for Auburn who was the first pick of the Chicago White Sox of the 1989 amateur draft.

773. In what city is the hit television show "Dexter" based?

774. In the Tour de France, what color jacket is worn by the winners of each stage?

775. In the spring of 1985, the No.1 song in America was "Don't You Forget About Me" from the soundtrack of "The Breakfast Club." Name the band that performed it.

776. Name the only American city with a population of over 500,000 from which you can drive south into Canada?

Answers

770) George Strait

771) Bret Favre

772) Frank Thomas

773) Miami

774) Yellow

775) Simple Minds

776) Detroit, Michigan

771- The first choice of the Farrelly brothers was to use Drew Bledsoe in this role, but he declined. They then asked Steve Young, who said he wouldn't be a part of a rated "R" movie.

777. Which U.S. Constitutional amendment lowered to voting age to 18?

778. Fill in the blank from this famous line from the movie "Dirty Harry:" "You got to ask yourself one question punk: 'Do I feel _____?'"

779. Name the only mammal that has the ability to fly.

780. In medical terminology, the prefix "hepato" refers to which organ?

781. In 1994, Jim Carrey released three blockbuster films: "Ace Ventura: Pet Detective," "Dumb and Dumber" and _____.

782. The highest-rated non-sporting event in television history was a 1983 episode of which show?

783. Name the 1988 film which became the first movie ever directed by a woman to gross over $100 million.

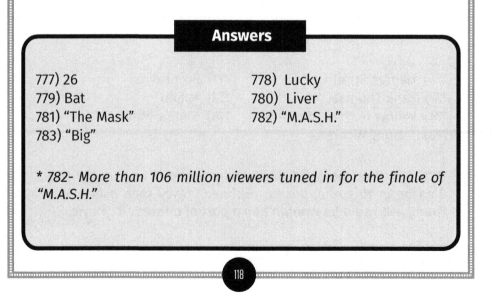

Answers

777) 26
779) Bat
781) "The Mask"
783) "Big"

778) Lucky
780) Liver
782) "M.A.S.H."

782- More than 106 million viewers tuned in for the finale of "M.A.S.H."

118

784. On the show "The Jetsons," what is the name of George and Jane Jetson's daughter?

785. Name the actress who played a teenager possessed by the devil in the 1973 film "The Exorcist."

786. What popular 70's and 80's sitcom featured characters named Jack and Larry hanging out at a club called the "Regal Beagle?"

787. What is the first name of the title character on the long-running medical drama, "Grey's Anatomy?"

788. Name the type of doll that caused near-riots to break out at malls across America in the Christmas season of 1983 because of the very high demand for them.

789. Name the future rock legend who was born on September 5, 1946, with the original name Farrokh Bulsara.

790. Name the 1985 movie starring Gregory Hines and Mikhail Barishnykov about Russian and American dancers becoming friends.

Answers

784. Judy
786. "Three's Company"
788. Cabbage Patch Kids
790. "White Nights"

785. Linda Blair
787. Meredith
789. Freddie Mercury

789- Mercury was born in the British protectorate of Zanzibar, which is now Tanzania

791. The fifth-largest city in the world spans two continents. Name it.

792. Veins carry blood to the heart. What carries blood away from the heart?

793. Name the boy band which sold more than two million copies of its album, "Home for Christmas," in 1998.

794. Name the 1948 short story by Shirley Jackson about a fictional town in mid-America which each year selects one community member to be stoned to death.

795. Name the actor who hosts a series on Disney Plus named after him called "The World According to _____."

796. What was the nickname of the Confederate general Thomas Jackson?

797. Name the 1968 film in which John Wayne plays Colonel Mike Kirby leading special forces in South Vietnam.

Answers

790) Istanbul   792) Arteries
793) N Sync   794) "The Lottery"
795) Jeff Goldblum   796) Stonewall
797) "The Green Berets"

791- Istanbul, Turkey, and its environs are in Europe, but the rest of Turkey is in Asia.

798. Name the first person to ever be named Sportsperson of the Year twice by "Sports Illustrated."

799. In what city is rock music legend Jim Morrison buried?

800. The song "My Heart Will Go On" by Celine Deon was featured on the soundtrack of which popular 1997 movie?

801. Name the artist who gained worldwide fame with paintings of Coke bottles and soup cans.

802. Who, at the age of 88 in 2010, became the oldest person ever to host "Saturday Night Live?"

803. What does the M in M.R.I. stand for?

804. Name the author who wrote "To Kill a Mockingbird."

Answers

798) Tiger Woods
800) "Titanic"
802) Betty White
804) Harper Lee

799) Paris
801) Andy Warhol
803) Magnetic

802- Miskel Spillman, at age 80, was the second oldest. She won a contest called "Anyone Can Host" held by N.B.C.

805. Name the 1972 hit by the band Deep Purple that was called by "Rolling Stone Magazine" the 11th-greatest hard rock song of all time.

806. Name the actress who was nominated 5 times for best actress, won the award in 1954 for her role in the movie "Roman Holiday," and also once raised money for the Nazi resistance by doing ballet.

807. Name the only U.S. state that shares no letters with its state capital.

808. In which country would one find Tiananmen Square?

809. As of 2020, which Big Ten school has won the most NCAA hockey championships?

810. Who was the only person to serve as both vice president and president of the United States without being elected to either position?

811. Name the country music singer who was born in Oklahoma in 1983 and first gained national attention by winning the fourth American Idol.

Answers

805) "Smoke on the Water"   806) Audrey Hepburn
807) South Dakota   808) China
809) University of Michigan   810) Gerald Ford
811) Carrie Underwood

810-Gerald Ford became vice president when Spiro Agnew resigned, then ascended to the presidency when Richard Nixon resigned.

812. Which insurance company did a man named Jake begin representing in 2011?

813. What is the nickname for professional wrestler Steve Austin?

814. Which Steven Spielberg film was the highest grossing movie of the 1980's?

815. Name the U.S. president who declared the very first "Mother's Day" in 1914.

816. On which state's license plate would you see the words "Grand Canyon State?"

817. In the movie " Top Gun," the character played by Tom Cruise has the call sign "Maverick." What is the call sign of his partner, played by Anthony Edwards?

818. Name the lead singer of the band "Fall Out Boy" who was once married to Ashley Simpson.

Answers

812) State Farm
814) "E.T."
816) Arizona
818) Pete Wentz

813) Stone Cold
815) Woodrow Wilson
817) Goose

814- Spielberg's highest grossing film of all time, when adjusted for inflation, is "Jaws."

819. Name the former third basemen who was the only player in Major League Baseball history to win batting titles in three different decades.

820. Which financial institution uses the slogan, "What's in your wallet?"

821. In which southern state is the 2000 film "O Brother, Where Art Thou?" set?

822. Richard Dawson, Louis Anderson, and Steve Harvey have all served as hosts of what popular game show?

823. Name the show aired on MTV from 2002 to 2005 about the domestic life of a heavy metal legend and his family.

824. Which state contains the most national parks?

825. In Billy Joel's 1973 hit "Piano Man," what is the first name of the man Paul is holding a conversation with?

Answers

819) George Brett

821) Mississippi

823) "The Osbournes"

825) Davy

820) Capital One

822) "Family Feud"

824) California

824- California has nine, Alaska has eight, Utah has five.

826. In "How the Grinch Stole Christmas," from what town does the Grinch steal Christmas items?

827. Name the sitcom which debuted in 2017 and is a spinoff of "The Big Bang Theory."

828. As of 2020, which city has hosted the most Super Bowls?

829. What was the name of the Obama family's dog when they lived in the White House?

830. Located partially in Arizona and partially in Utah, this lake trails only Lake Mead in terms of largest man-made reservoirs in the United States.

831. Name the rapper whose girlfriend Eryikah Badu appeared in his music video titled "The Light."

832. What does the number of carats designated on a diamond indicate?

Answers

826) Whoville
828) Miami
830) Lake Powell
832) Weight

827) "Young Sheldon"
829) Bo
831) Common

828- Miami has hosted 11, New Orleans:10, Los Angeles:7

833. What does the 19 indicate in the disease "COVID-19?"

834. Who was the first Major League Baseball player to earn $1 million in a season?

835. In packages of M&M's, which color is featured the least?

836. As of 2020, which NBA team plays its games in the oldest arena?

837. Name the four-time country music entertainer of the year who released his seventh studio album in 2020 titled "Born Here Live Here Die Here?"

838. Who was the first U.S. president to preside over 50 states?

839. With speeds of 40 mph, what is the fastest ride in Disneyland?

Answers

833) The year 2019
834) Brown
837) Luke Bryan
839) Splash Mountain

834) Nolan Ryan
836) New York Knicks
838) Dwight Eisenhower

*833- "Covid 19"= "Co" represents corona , "vi "represents virus, "d "represents disease, "19" represents 2019

840. Who was named the NBA MVP in 1984, 1985, and 1986?

841. If you travelled west across the Ural Mountains, you would travel into which continent?

842. The name of which U.S. state means "Green Mountain" in French?

843. Name the movie which won multiple Academy Awards and ends with the line, "After all, tomorrow is another day."

844. Name the popular comic strip cat created by Jim Davis in 1978.

845. Gillian Anderson played Special Agent Dana Scully on what popular science fiction television drama?

846. Name the Canadian singer whose hits include "Wicked Games," "The Hills," and "Call Out My Name."

Answers

840) Larry Bird
842) Vermont
844) Garfield
846) The Weekend

841) Europe
843) "Gone With the Wind'
845) "X Files"

847. Which hotel on the Las Vegas strip features an eight-acre lake with dancing fountains?

848. In the 1976 movie "The Bad News Bears," which actor plays the role of coach Morris Buttermaker?

849. There are three members of the animated singing group "The Chipmunks." One is Alvin, and another is Simon. What is the first name of the third chipmunk?

850. Name the classic rock band whose hits included "Lola," "You Really Got Me," and "All Day and All of the Night."

851. "The Last Dance" is a documentary released in 2020 about which professional sports team?

852. Between 1999 and 2001, what NFL running back won the NFL's offensive player of the year award three consecutive times?

853. Which band is known by the last name of three brothers named Kevin, Joe, and Nick?

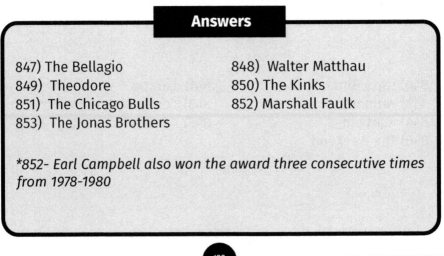

Answers

847) The Bellagio
849) Theodore
851) The Chicago Bulls
853) The Jonas Brothers

848) Walter Matthau
850) The Kinks
852) Marshall Faulk

852- Earl Campbell also won the award three consecutive times from 1978-1980

854. Name the original host of "Who Wants to Be a Millionaire?" who passed away in 2020.

855. Name the actress nominated for the Oscar award for best actress four times between 1991 to 1996, The films she was nominated for were "Thelma and Louise," "Lorenzo's Oil," "The Client," and "Dead Man Walking."

856. Name the pop singer born in Barbados who released her debut album in 2005 titled "Music of the Sun."

857. At Texas A&M University, what does the A stand for?

858. "The Curse of the Bambino" is said to have afflicted which Major League Baseball team from 1918 to 2004?

859. How many seasons of college basketball did Kobe Bryant play?

860. Name the 2008 film about two salesmen for the energy drink Minotaur who get into trouble and have to work with at-risk youth.

Answers

854) Regis Philbin   855.) Susan Sarandon
856) Rihanna   857) Agriculture
858) Boston Red Sox   859) Zero
860) "Role Models"

857- A and M stands for Agricultural and Mechanical

861. Name the popular but raunchy animated comedy series about adolescence created by Nick Kroll which debuted on Netflix in 2017.

862. "Californication," "Higher Ground," and "Aeroplane" are all hits recorded by what popular alternative rock band?

863. Which state produces about 8 million Christmas trees a year, the most of any in America?

864. Who has won more Olympic medals than any other athlete in history?

865. What was the name of the treaty which ended World War One?

866. Name the Eagles song which begins with the lyrics "Raven hair and ruby lips, sparks fly from her fingertips."

867. In which American city will you find both O'Hare and Midway international airports?

Answers

861) "Big Mouth"

862) The Red Hot Chili Peppers

863) Oregon

864) Michael Phelps

865) Treaty of Versailles

866) "Witchy Woman"

867) Chicago

864- Michael Phelps won 28, Soviet gymnast Larisa Latynina is second with 18.

868. Name the former University of Alabama quarterback that led the New York Jets to a Superbowl championship in what is considered to be the greatest upset in that game's history.

869. Santiago is the capital city of what South American country?

870. Name the popular app in which users often share short videos featuring dancing and singing which was downloaded 45 million times in the first three months of 2018.

871. Name the television series which often featured the "Vulcan salute" accompanied with the phrase "live long and prosper."

872. Name the former member of the cast of "Friends" who was the first-ever guest on "The Ellen DeGeneres Show" in 2003.

873. The most reproduced photograph of all time is of six U.S. Marines hoisting a flag on which island?

874. Name the famous ancient leader who wrote home to say, "I came, I saw, I conquered"

Answers

868) Joe Namath
870) Tik Tok
872) Jennifer Aniston
874) Julius Caesar

869) Chile
871) "Star Trek"
873) Iwo Jima

875. Released in 1997, the first Harry Potter book was titled "Harry Potter and the _____"

876. Which amendment to the United States Constitution granted women the right to vote in 1920?

877. Name the heavy metal band whose albums include "The Battle of Los Angeles" and "Evil Empire."

878. Who is the second African-American to serve on the United States Supreme Court?

879. Who wrote the popular novels "The Da Vinci Code" and "Angels and Demons?"

880. Give the last name of the only father-son combination to ever hit back-to-back home runs in the major leagues.

881. Name the popular series aired on Hulu about a fictional totalitarian state in the future named "Gilead."

Answers

875) Philosopher's Stone   876. 19th
877) Rage Against The Machine   878) Clarence Thomas
879) Dan Brown   880) Griffey
881) A Handmaid's Tale

878- Clarence Thomas was nominated by George H.W. Bush July 1, 1991.

882. Only two artists have had five No. 1 singles from the same album. One was Michael Jackson. Who was the other?

883. This drinking term is believed to have been invented in the Navy in the early 1900s. It is illegal in 8 states, but thoroughly enjoyed on many afternoons in the other 42. Name it.

884. Patricia Krenwinkel, Linda Kasabian, and Susan Atkins were all members of what murderous "family?"

885. What is the nickname of the national hockey league team which represents New Jersey?

886. Name the female artist whose 2017 song "Praying' was nominated for the Grammy best pop solo performance.

887. Name the actor who starred as Norman Bates in the original "Psycho."

888. Name the Colorado resort city which was named after the abundance of trees which grow in the area.

Answers

882) Katy Perry

883) Happy Hour

884) Manson Family

885) Devils

886) Kesha

887) Anthony Perkins

888) Aspen

882- Katy Perry's album "Teenage Dream" had the No. 1 hits: "California Gurls," "Firework," "Teenage Dream," "Last Friday Night (T.G.I.F.)," and "E.T."

889. Name the drug intended to help pregnant moms with morning sickness which caused tens of thousands of babies to be born with defects in the early 1960s.

890. In 1993, there were three members of the Mickey Mouse Club who would go on to be superstars. They were Britney Spears, Justin Timberlake, and who?

891. In October 1975, which singer became the first rock star ever to be featured on the covers of both "Time" and "Newsweek" magazines in the same week?

892. Name the country which celebrates "Bastille Day" each July.

893. One of the most famous scenes in the history of television is from the show "I Love Lucy," when Lucy and her friend Ethel get a job at a _____ factory.

894. The Korean pop sensation known as PSY became a viral sensation in 2012 with his hit _____.

895. Which state is nicknamed "The Peach State?"

Answers

889) Thalidomide
891) Bruce Springsteen
893) Chocolate
895) Georgia

890) Christina Aguilera
892) France
894) Gangnam Style

889- Francis Oldham Kelsey is credited with blocking the use of thalidomide in the United States. The headquarters of the F.D.A. is now named after her.

896. Name the movie released in 2019, which passed "The Lion King" to become the highest grossing animated film of all time.

897. Name the actress who made her big screen debut in the 1978 movie "Halloween" as the character Laurie Strode?

898. Name the 1993 film which starred Val Kimer as Doc Holliday and Kurt Russell as Wyatt Earp.

899. Ghostface Killah, Rza, 'Ol Dirty Bastard, Gza, and Method Man were all members of what legendary rap group?

900. Name the player who in 2003, while playing for the Lakers, became the oldest player ever to have a triple-double in an NBA game.

901. "I was 12 going on 13 the first time I saw a dead human being," is the opening line to what 1986 movie?

902. Name the famous serial killer who was executed in Florida on January 24, 1989.

Answers

896) "Frozen 2"
898) "Tombstone"
900) Karl Malone
902) Ted Bundy

897) Jamie Lee Curtis
899) Wu Tang Clan
901) "Stand By Me"

900- Malone was 40 years, 127 days old when he had 10 points, 11 rebounds, and 10 assists against the Spurs.

903. Which band made nightly calls to President George H.W. Bush as part of their 1992 "Zoo TV" tour?

904. Name the second baseman for the Boston Red Sox who won the 2008 American League MVP award.

905. When Larry the Cable Guy, Bill Engvall, Ron White, and Jeff Foxworthy perform together, what are they known as?

906. Name the 1999 movie in which John Voight played a Texas high school football coach named Bud Kilmer.

907. Name the children's show on Nickelodeon which starred Steve Burns from 1996 to 2002, and Donavon Patton from 2002 to 2006.

908. Name the comedian who is best known for his portrayal of Fred Sanford in the television show "Sanford and Son"

909. Name the actress who won the Academy Award for best actress for her role in "Silver Linings Playbook" but tripped on her way to the stage to accept the award.

Answers

903) U2

904) Dustin Pedroia

905) Blue Collar Comedy Tour

906) Varsity Blues

907) "Blues Clues"

908) Red Foxx

909) Jennifer Lawrence

910. What is the nickname for the athletic teams at DePaul University?

911. Name the 1982 Billy Idol song that begins with the line "Hey little sister what have you done?"

912. Name the artist who in 2015 asked us to watch him whip and nae nae.

913. What did the Kelly Car Company begin publishing in 1918 to help establish the value of used cars?

914. Name the British comedy group whose films include "The Holy Grail," "The Meaning of Life," "Flying Circus", and "Life of Brian."

915. The third "Star Wars" film was released May 25th, 1983. What was the name of that movie?

916. Name the former first basemen for the Cubs and Diamondbacks who led the Major Leagues in hits in the 1990s.

Answers

910) Blue Demons
912) Silento
914) Monty Python
916) Mark Grace

911) "White Wedding"
913) Blue Book
915) "Return of the Jedi"

914- "Monty Python" was not an individual but a comedy troupe of six original members.

917. Willie Mosconi and Minnesota Fats are considered to be two of the greatest players ever at what sport?

918. In the show "Everybody Loves Raymond," what does Raymond do for a living?

919. Name the sitcom which aired on NBC from 1991 to 1997 featuring Brian and Joe Hackett as brothers and pilots in Nantucket, Massachusetts?

920. In terms of the outdoor gear store, what do the letters REI stand for?

921. Which Ivy League school is located in Ithaca, New York?

922. In 2015, which host of the Miss Universe award show famously announced the wrong winner?

923. There are three state capitals that begin with the letter P. Which one is furthest east?

Answers

917) Pool/billiards
919) "Wings" Incorporated
921) Cornell
923) Providence

918) Newspaper reporter
920) Recreational Equipment
922) Steve Harvey

923- The three state capitals that start with "P" are Providence, Phoenix, and Pierre.

924. Name the anti-war novel written by Kurt Vonnegut, released in 1969, following the life of Billy Pilgrim.

925. Name the singer whose nicknames include "Old Blue Eyes" and "The Chairman of the Board."

926. Name the racquet sport played by two or four players played with a small, hollow rubber ball, smaller than the one used in racquetball.

927. Name the two time Olympic gold medal winning women's soccer player who married former Major League all-star Nomar Garciappara.

928. Give the title to the song by Sister Sledge which went to No. 1 on the R&B charts and was the theme song to the world champion Pittsburgh Pirates in 1979.

929. Name the 2003 movie starring Will Ferrell in which he wreaks havoc in New York City because of his abnormal size and child-like behavior.

930. Name the viral dance that "Backpack Kid" introduced to the world in 2017.

Answers

923) "Slaughterhouse Five"   925) Frank Sinatra
926) Squash   927) Mia Hamm
928) "We Are Family"   929) "Elf"
930) The Floss

931. Which state is nicknamed the "Bluegrass State?"

932. Before moving to Arizona, in what city did the Cardinals of the NFL play their home games?

933. What is the name of the Greek god of the underworld?

934. In 2019, which brand led the world in vodka sales?

935. In the movie "Ace Ventura Pet Detective" What was the name of the dolphin that was kidnapped?

936. Name the popular musical set in Russia in 1905 based on the story of Tevye and his daughters.

937. Name the television show that tells the story of Michael Bluth, who takes over family affairs after his father goes to prison.

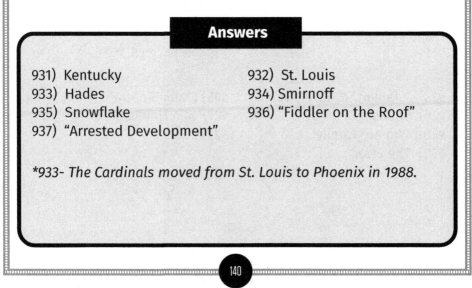

Answers

931) Kentucky
933) Hades
935) Snowflake
937) "Arrested Development"

932) St. Louis
934) Smirnoff
936) "Fiddler on the Roof"

933- The Cardinals moved from St. Louis to Phoenix in 1988.

938. What did the restaurant chain "I.H.O.P." briefly change its name to in 2018?

939. In the movie 'Tommy Boy," from which university does Tommy graduate?

940. On which network did the shows "Married With Children," "The Simpsons," and "Family Guy" all make their debut?

941. All radio stations west of the Mississippi start with the call letter "K." With what letter do those east of the Mississippi start?

942. What was the name of the 1984 movie starring Molly Ringwald and Anthony Michael Hall about a girl whose birthday is forgotten?

943. In 1994, Wayne Gretzky broke the record for most career goals for the NHL. Which team was he with when he broke this record?

944. In 2019, thousands of people went to storm the mysterious land known as "Area 51." What state is it in?

Answers

938) I.H.O.B.
940) Fox
942) "Sixteen Candles"
944) Nevada

939) Marquette
941) W
943) Los Angeles Kings

938- I.H.O.P. turned the "P" upside down for a few weeks to promote sales of their hamburgers.

945. What state did John McCain represent in the United States Senate?

946. In December of 1999, who did "Time Magazine" name as its "Person of the Century?"

947. Who was the former Yankee who was the only person in baseball history to win 10 World Series rings as a player?

948. What does the computer acronym U.R.L. stand for?

949. In 2013, Norwegian comedy duo Ylvis, comprised of brothers Vegard and Bård Ylvisåker, rose to prominence after releasing the viral hit asking a question about what type of animal?

950. Name the 1979 film in which Bill Murray made his big screen debut as a head counselor at a summer camp.

951. Name the Kentucky straight bourbon whiskey whose nicknames include "The Dirty Bird" and " Bombed Tom."

Answers

945) Arizona

946) Albert Einstein

947) Yogi Berra

948) Uniformed Resource Locator

949) Fox

950) "Meatballs"

951) Wild Turkey

947- Joe DiMaggio is second, with nine world series rings as a player.

952. What is the only metal that is liquid at room temperature?

953. Who in 2014 "broke the Internet" with her picture on the cover of "Paper" magazine?

954. In terms of square mileage, which is the smallest of America's fifty states?

955. Nolan Ryan struck out more batters than any other pitcher in major league history. Name the pitcher who struck out the second-most.

956. Name the 1978 film in which the band Otis Day and the Nights are featured singing the songs "Shout" and "Shama Lama Ding Dong."

957. Name the nurse that is credited with founding the American Red Cross.

958. Name the 2006 movie about a battle in 480 B.C. against invading Persians in the mountain pass of Thermopylae.

Answers

952) Mercury

953) Kim Kardashian

954) Rhode Island

955) Randy Johnson

956) "Animal House"

957) Clara Barton

958) "300"

954- Delaware is the second smallest state, followed by Connecticut and Hawaii.

959. When Bob Dole ran for President as the Republican nominee in 1996, who was his running mate?

960. In 2019, the hashtag "#metoo" exploded in force after allegations against which Hollywood producer were leveled by Alyssa Milano?

961. In the popular expression "Mind your P's and Q's," what do the P and Q stand for?

962. Karch Kiraly led the U.S. Olympic team to two gold medals in which sport?

963. What travel company did William Shatner serve as pitchman for two decades?

964. Name the NBA player who played his college basketball for the Naval Academy and was named the 1989-1990 rookie of the year and would later be named one of the 50 greatest NBA players of all time.

965. Whose 1993 autobiography titled "Private Parts" was released as a movie in 1997?

Answers

959) Jack Kemp
961) Pints and Quarts
963) Priceline
965) Howard Stern

960) Harvey Weinstein
962) Volleyball
964) David Robinson

961- There is some debate about this, as several other theories exist as well as to the origin of this phrase.

966. Name the woman who was married to Adolf Hitler for 40 hours before committing suicide with him in 1945.

967. Name the singer who reached No. 8 on the U.S. charts in 1984 with the song "Sunglasses at Night."

968. What real-life figure did Leonardo DiCaprio portray in the 2004 movie "The Aviator?"

969. What day of the year did presidents John Adams, Thomas Jefferson, and James Monroe all die on?

970. Elon Musk faced scrutiny when he smoked marijuana on whose popular pod cast in 2018?

971. Name the actress who played the character Gabrielle Solis on the "Desperate Housewives" series.

972. Which popular singer did Hailey Baldwin marry in 2018?

Answers

966) Eva Braun
968) Howard Hughes
970) Joe Rogan
972) Justin Bieber

967) Corey Hart
969) July 4
971) Eva Longoria

969- Adams and Jefferson died hours apart on July 4, 1826; the 50th anniversary of the signing of the Declaration of Independence.

973. In what country was the Nazi concentration camp known as Auschwitz?

974. Name the 1988 movie starring Steve Martin and Michael Caine as a big time and small time con men competing against each other in France?

975. Former Seahawks great Steve Largent served in the United States House of Representatives from 1994 to 2002. What state did he represent?

976. Name the female singer whose debut album in 1996 "Tidal" included the hits "Sleep To Dream," "Shadow Boxer," and "Criminal."

977. Which Major League Baseball team's uniforms feature an elephant?

978. Name the actor who starred as the character Philo Beddoe in the movies "Every Which Way but Loose" and its sequel "Any Which Way You Can."

979. The late James Gandolfini was best known for his role as a gangster named Tony on what former HBO series?

Answers

973) Poland

974) "Dirty Rotten Scoundrels"

975) Oklahoma

976) Fiona Apple

977) Oakland Athletics

978) Clint Eastwood

979) "The Sopranos"

980. What team did Alex Rodriguez play for in between being a Mariner and a Yankee?

981. Name the actress who played Sally in the 1989 movie "When Harry met Sally?"

982. Name the country music solo artist who was once the lead singer of the band "Hootie and the Blowfish."

983. In "High School Musical," what is the name of the high school?

984. Who was the first American president to be impeached?

985. Name the band whose 1999 single "Nookie" made the top ten on both the rap and the rock charts.

986. In the 1987 movie, "Planes, Trains, and Automobiles," to what city are Steve Martin and John Candy trying to get for Thanksgiving weekend?

Answers

980) Texas Rangers   981) Meg Ryan
982) Darius Rucker   983) East High
984) Andrew Johnson   985) Limp Bizkit
986) Chicago

984- In total, three United States presidents have been impeached. In each case, the Senate voted not to convict. The other two are Bill Clinton and Donald Trump.

987. Name the Neil Young album which includes the songs "Old Man" and "Heart of Gold," that was the top selling album of 1972.

988. What is the more common name of the plant Phorandendron serotinum, which you should only stand under if you want to be kissed?

989. Who was the mayor of New York City on September 11, 2001?

990. Name the NBA team that won back-to-back championships in 1989 and 1990, and was named by "Sports illustrated" as the most hated team in professional team sports history.

991. Name the movie released in 2001 that is a psychological fantasy thriller starring Drew Barrymore, Patrick Swayze, and Jake Gyllenhal.

992. For which NFL team did Joe Montana play his last game in 1993?

993. Name the award winning P.B.S. filmmaker who produced the series "The Civil War," "Baseball," and "Jazz."

Answers

987) "Harvest"
989) Rudy Guliani
991) Donnie Darko
993) Ken Burns

988) Mistletoe
990) Detroit Pistons
992) Kansas City Chiefs

990 The 1992/93 Dallas Cowboys were the second most hated team on Sports Illustrated's list.

994. Name the pop duo who had a hit in 1972 with "Summer Breeze."

995. Name the former New York Mets first baseman who appeared in a cameo on "Seinfeld" as a love interest of Elaine's in 1992.

996. What scale is used to measure the intensity of earthquakes?

997. Name the 1985 Chevy Chase film in which Chevy plays a Lakers fan who writes a column under the name "Jane Doe" while making up multiple identities to gather information.

998. Name the quarterback who won the 1984 Heisman Trophy while playing for Boston College.

999. In 1995, Cal Ripken broke the record for most consecutive games played by a major league baseball player. Whose record did he break?

1000. Name the actor whose movie credits include "Major League," "Passenger 57," "U.S. Marshalls," and "Blade."

Answers

994) Seals and Croft
996) Richter
998) Doug Flutie
1000) Wesley Snipes

995) Keith Hernandez
997) "Fletch"
999) Lou Gehrig

Coming in December 2020:

"Timeless Trivia Volume II"

To quench your trivia fix until then, follow "Timelesstrivia" on Instagram, Facebook and Twitter

Made in the USA
Middletown, DE
29 May 2021